CITY SCHOOL ATTENDANCE SERVICE

BY

FREDERICK EARLE EMMONS, Ph.D.

TEACHERS COLLEGE, COLUMBIA UNIVERSITY
CONTRIBUTIONS TO EDUCATION, No. 200

BUREAU OF PUBLICATIONS
Teachers College, Columbia University
NEW YORK CITY
1926

Printed in the United States of America by
J. J. LITTLE AND IVES COMPANY, NEW YORK

ACKNOWLEDGMENT

As one looks back over the paths along which he has come to the completion of a task like this, he finds many who have offered helping hands and words of advice.

To the chairman of my Committee, Dr. George D. Strayer, do I especially wish to express my sincere gratitude for his many valuable suggestions and his unceasing encouragement. To Dr. Paul Mort, Dr. David Snedden, Dr. E. S. Evenden, Dr. J. McGaughy, and Dr. N. L. Engelhardt, who at every opportunity gave freely of their time during the progress of the study, the writer feels deeply indebted.

In the cities visited, the Superintendents of Schools and particularly the Attendance Officers have most cordially assisted in securing the data necessary for this study. To them the author is under obligation.

To my wife, Mary F. Emmons, who during the years of postgraduate study has willingly borne the sacrifice so often required and who has shown untiring devotion to the completion of this task I can only slightly express my deep appreciation.

F. E. E.

CONTENTS

Contents

LIST OF FORMS RECOMMENDED

TABLES AND CHARTS

TABLES

CHARTS

INTRODUCTION

The progress of compulsory education has now reached the levels where there is increasing interest in the enforcement of existing laws rather than in the further enactment of new ones. For years investigations and reports have shown that laws for greater efficiency in school attendance are not yet fully operative and that accurate child accounting is lacking.

Standards of instruction, supervision, and the many aspects of school administration have been advanced by the investigations of prevailing practices and the checking of these practices with accepted standards now existing or proposed. With the opportunities for education thus improved greater consideration should now be given to assuring the child of school age of regular contact with them.

THE PURPOSE OF THIS STUDY

The purpose of this investigation has been (*a*) to determine the actual attendance service in a number of typical cities in several states, (*b*) to determine wherein this service failed to meet the necessary standards for the organization, administration, and effectiveness of a modern attendance service, and (*c*) in the light of the personal investigations made, the reports and surveys of the many cities studied, to outline methods by which attendance service may function more efficiently.

SOURCES OF DATA

In order to carry out this investigation a detailed study was made of the 1923–24 attendance reports of fifty cities from all sections of the United States. Important city school surveys have been carefully examined for any contributions that might lend a more extensive outlook to the study.

The most important task, however, was to gain first-hand information regarding actual existing conditions. Fifteen cities were selected, eleven of which were within reasonable distance of

New York City, so that constant personal contact might be maintained for a period of several months and numerous visits made to investigate the actual workings of the attendance service, to examine records and reports, and to study the routines of procedure that could not be fully analyzed by a single visit or conference with the school authorities. In each of the other cities several days were spent in a complete survey of the attendance service.

With the exception of a few instances the names of the cities are not given because it was only after a promise to the attendance officers and superintendents not to mention the city by name that the writer was able to secure a frank disclosure of the actual workings of the department as well as full access to all the details of the attendance service.

In the fifteen cities selected we have cities in Massachusetts, New York, Pennsylvania, Connecticut, Rhode Island, Ohio, and New Jersey, states with varying degrees of control over attendance service. The cities are of typical urban conditions, industrial, commercial, with large foreign-born population and large native element, and with nearby agricultural sections. In cities not visited there may be a difference in the difficulty of the attendance problem due to racial, economic and environmental conditions, but methods necessary for efficient organization and administration of attendance service should not be very different from those of the cities studied. In other words, the quantity of the task may vary but the quality should have the same goal as a minimum,—that every child of compulsory school age shall be in school every day unless legally excused.

Because of the number and type of the cities chosen and the intensive study made of these cities and because of visits to many other cities in order to get at the innermost workings of the attendance service, it is believed that such a study makes a real contribution to our knowledge of attendance service. This should result in a more general realization that we are just beginning to see clearly a distinct and important administrative problem. It demands a more scientific child-accounting practice if we are to offer a practical means to bring attendance service to a degree of efficiency more comparable to the other phases of school administration.

The results of the investigations are presented under the following headings:

1. Administration and Organization.
2. Registration of School Population.
3. Regularity of Attendance.
4. Attendance Service and the Courts.
5. Attendance Service and Child Employment.

CITY SCHOOL ATTENDANCE SERVICE

CHAPTER I

THE BACKGROUND FOR THE STUDY OF ATTENDANCE SERVICE

HISTORICAL FOUNDATION

The principle of compulsory education now so universal in this country has its origin in Old World customs and laws. The early settlers in the country were already (imbued) with the conviction that it was a religious duty to see that every child was taught to read.

A little more than twenty years after the landing of the Pilgrim Fathers in 1642, the general court of Massachusetts issued an order that instruction be given in certain subjects.[1] The failure of this order to prescribe where the children should be taught was remedied five years later (1647) when elementary and secondary schools were made compulsory and their support by taxation ordered.[2]

In these two laws are embodied all but two of the principles upon which the present conception of compulsory education rests: (*a*) that all children should be educated, (*b*) that the parent or community must make provision for such education, and (*c*) that it is the right of the state to enforce this obligation. Nearly all of these principles are to be found at least outlined in the measures offered and partially enforced in England during several centuries preceding the emigrations to America.[3]

The two elements of the modern compulsory education law that are not found in the early measures are an attendance requirement and restriction on child labor during the school period.

[1] *Records of Massachusetts Colony,* Vol. II, p. 6.
[2] *Ibid.,* Vol. II, p. 203.
[3] Ensign, F. C., *School Attendance and Child Labor,* p. 23.

The histories of the early colonies disclose the gradual development of the principle of compulsory education, but the records are silent as to the extent of its enforcement.[4] We may look to Massachusetts for the contribution of the law and to Connecticut for the contribution of its administration and methods of enforcement.

The failure of the towns in Connecticut and Massachusetts to maintain the promise of these earlier years is seen in the increased penalties of 1671 and 1683 in Massachusetts when the required schools were not provided. In Connecticut in 1700 and in Massachusetts in 1701 efforts were again made to secure more adequate administration by the reënactment of the former laws with new emphasis upon the support of the schools and upon the enforcement of the law.

The conditions of early pioneer life and the changing type of population brought a noticeable decline in the former standards. The apathy and non-enforcement continued until the new economic era of the nineteenth century with its developing spirit of democracy brought new aspirations for educational opportunity.

During the early decades of our national life the former colonies continued their educational standards in their new constitutions or statutes. The principle of compulsion, however, does not seem to be strongly emphasized.[5] The requirements as to the number of schools were less strict, and greater freedom was allowed the individual communities. With the coming of industrial development and the increasing urbanization of the population a new value was discovered in child employment. From this time on the compulsory education laws rest largely upon the laws to regulate child labor. Connecticut was a leader in the legislative programs that followed. Philanthropists registered their wishes but little or no attempt at enforcement was evident. By 1836 Massachusetts, under the rising influence of the working classes, now politically strengthened by manhood suffrage, sought to limit child labor and make educational provisions for them. Other states began to feel the same struggle of the working classes for recognition.

With varying degrees of success and failure up to the second decade of the twentieth century the states were compelled to over-

⁴ See Jernegan, "Compulsory Education in the American Colonies," *School Review*, 1918, pp. 704-44.
⁵ Steiner, *History of Education in Connecticut*, p. 35, Law of 1798.

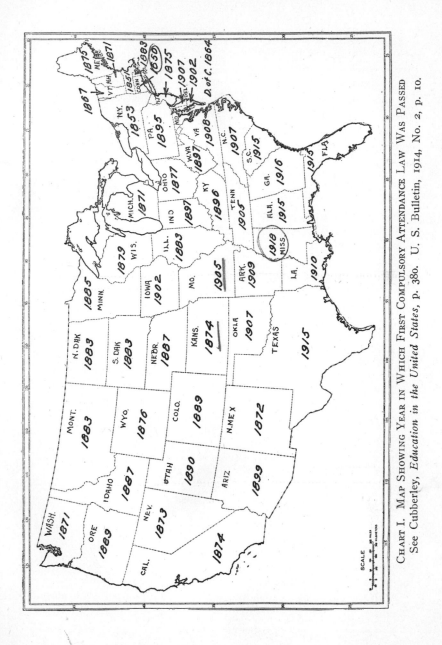

CHART I. MAP SHOWING YEAR IN WHICH FIRST COMPULSORY ATTENDANCE LAW WAS PASSED
See Cubberley, *Education in the United States*, p. 380. U. S. Bulletin, 1914, No. 2, p. 10.

3

come opposition on the part of those who argued that (*a*) the law was not necessary for good attendance, (*b*) it was an arrogation of new powers by the government, (*c*) it deprived the parent of inalienable rights, (*d*) it was not in keeping with the spirit of free democratic institutions.[6]

In Chart I we can see when each state passed its first compulsory attendance law. From three states on the Atlantic seaboard with only 4.9 per cent of population under compulsory attendance in 1870 we now find state authorities reaching out from one end of the country to the other with only three states leaving the control of compulsory education to varying extents in the power of the local authorities.[7]

It was nearly one hundred and fifty years after the founding of our democracy before all its commonwealths accepted their responsibilities and wrote laws in their statute books looking towards a complete acknowledgment of their duty.

PRESENT LEGAL STATUS OF SCHOOL ATTENDANCE

Chart II gives a graphic description of the present legal conception of compulsory education attained throughout the country, not alone by states but by geographic conditions. The light area shows the years of compulsory education. The dotted years show the present conception of what period should be open in the child's life to legal exploitation by parent, guardian or employer. It is in these years and in the years of the darkened area of the chart, which are now left to the option of the parent, that far-sighted educators see the pre-school, continuation and post-school educational possibilities. Even such a picture fails to tell the full story of the variations in educational status. The length of the school year, the inadequacy and inequality of educational opportunities and the part-time conditions lie hidden, only to be brought to light by the state and community surveys that, from time to time, are now disclosing what the words of statutes would tend to conceal.

Although nineteen states legally declare that nine years is the minimum period for the proper education of the child for its citizenship, eight states are willing to accept six years of schooling

---

[6] For further discussion see Diffenbaugh, W. S., *Compulsory Education in the U. S.,* Bureau of Education, Bul. 1914, No. 2, pp. 10-12.
[7] For total population and percentage of population under compulsory school attendance laws see Bixler, E. C., *An Investigation to Determine Efficiency with Which Compulsory Attendance Law Is Enforced in Philadelphia* (Table 1).

```
                 1 2 3 4 5 6 7 8 9 10 11 12 13 14 15 16 17 18 19 20
Eastern States (Industrial)
 1. Connecticut ████████████xxxxxxxxxxxxxxxxxx......███████████████
 2. Maine        ██████████xxxxxxxxxxxxxxxxxxxx...██████████████
 3. Mass.        ████████████xxxxxxxxxxxxxxxxxx......████████████
 4. New Jersey   ██████████xxxxxxxxxxxxxxxxxx......████████████
 5. N. Hampshire ████████████xxxxxxxxxxxxxxxx......████████████
 6. New York     ██████████xxxxxxxxxxxxxxxx......████████████
 7. Penna.       ████████████████████████████████████████████
 8. Rhode Island ██████████xxxxxxxxxxxxxxxxxx......███████████
 9. Vermont      ██████████xxxxxxxxxxxxxxxx......███████████
Southern States
10. Alabama      ████████████xxxxxxxxxxxxxxx......████████████
11. Arkansas     ██████████xxxxxxxxxxxxxxxx...██████████████
12. Delaware     ██████████xxxxxxxxxxxxxxxxxx.......███████████
13. Florida      ██████████xxxxxxxxxxxxxxxxxx......████████████
14. Georgia      ███████████xxxxxxxxxxx......████
15. Kentucky     ██████████xxxxxxxxxxxxxxxx......████████████
16. Louisiana    ██████████xxxxxxxxxxxxxxxxx████████████████
17. Maryland     ██████████xxxxxxxxxxxxxxxxxx......████████████
18. Miss.        ██████████xxxxxxxxxxxxxxxxx██████████████
19. N.Carolina   ██████████xxxxxxxxxxxxxxxx██████████████
20. S.Carolina   ██████████xxxxxxxxxxxxxxxx████████████████
21. Tennessee    ██████████xxxxxxxxxxxxxxxxxx........
22. Texas        ██████████xxxxxxxxx......████████████████
23. Virginia     ██████████xxxxxxxxxxxxxxxx██████████████
24. W.Virginia   ██████████xxxxxxxxxxxxxxxxxx......████████████
Great Lake States (Manufacturing)
25. Illinois     ██████████xxxxxxxxxxxxxxxxxx......███████████
26. Indiana      ██████████xxxxxxxxxxxxxxxxx......████████████
27. Michigan     ██████████xxxxxxxxxxxxxxxxxxxx...███████████
28. Ohio         ████████xxxxxxxxxxxxxxxxxxxxxxxxxxxx......█.
29. Wisconsin    ████████xxxxxxxxxxxxxxxxx.......
Great Plain States (Agricultural)
30. Iowa         ██████████xxxxxxxxxxxxxxxxx......████████████
31. Kansas       ██████████xxxxxxxxxxxxxxx......████████████
32. Minnesota    ████████████xxxxxxxxxxxxxx......████████████
33. Missouri     ██████████xxxxxxxxxxxxxxxxx......█████████████
34. Nebraska     ██████████xxxxxxxxxxxxxxxxx......████████████
35. N.Dakota     ██████████xxxxxxxxxxxxxxxxx.......
36. Oklahoma     ██████████xxxxxxxxxxxxxxxxxxxxxxx......████
37. S.Dakota     ██████████xxxxxxxxxxxxxxxx......████████████
Western States
38. Arizona      ████████████xxxxxxxxxxxxxxxx......████████████
39. Calif.       ████████████xxxxxxxxxxxxxxxx......██████
40. Colorado     ██████████xxxxxxxxxxxxxxxx......████████████
41. Idaho        ████████████xxxxxxxxxxxxxxxx......████████████
42. Montana      ████████████xxxxxxxxxxxxxxx......████████████
43. Nevada       ██████████xxxxxxxxxxxxxxxx......████████████
44. New Mexico   ██████████xxxxxxxxxxxxxxxxxx.......████████
45. Oregon       ██████████xxxxxxxxxxxxxxxx......
46. Utah         ██████████xxxxxxxxxxxxxxxxxxxxx......████████
47. Wash.        ██████████xxxxxxxxxxxxxxx......████████████
48. Wyoming      ██████████xxxxxxxxxxxxxxxxx██
```

CHART II. COMPULSORY SCHOOL ATTENDANCE AND CHILD EMPLOYMENT
AGE—THE UNITED STATES BY STATES AND GEOGRAPHIC DIVISIONS

████ Non-Compulsory Years.   xxx Compulsory Years
.... Legal Employment Ages

Research Bulletin, N. E. A., Vol. No. 4, Sept. 1923, p. 259.

For division by states, see Evenden, E. S., Teachers' Salaries and Salary Schedules, N. E. A. Commission Series No. 6, 1919, p. 9.

for those who will exercise its franchise. Two states in the western area seek ten years as the legal requirement. The lower age limit of seven years is operative in fifty per cent of the states, while all the others, with the exception of three, accept an eight-year entrance age. Many children, no doubt, in these states enter school before they are eight years old, but the local community and the parent, rather than the state, must take the initiative in seeking the opportunity of starting the child at an earlier age. The upper age limit shows a greater uniformity of accepted standards. Thirty-four states declare that sixteen years should be the age at which the state should no longer exercise compulsory control. These states, however, by the two-year optional period of child labor and by the careless supervision of its operations, shorten the educational span. The two states that are now making eighteen years the upper age limit are, to that extent, offering an educational program considered desirable by many educators.

In actual conditions over the last fifty years the extent to which we have attained the prevailing ideal is shown in the national statistics for each decade.[8] Such figures, gradually growing towards higher levels, appear as encouraging signs of our national attitude toward education. The total per cent of population enrolled in schools has increased from 17.8 per cent to 21.3 per cent. The gain in the average number of days the schools were in session rose from 132.2 per cent in 1870 to 144.3 per cent in 1900. The average effective school year in the United States is 130.6 days out of an average of 164 days the schools are in session. If the time necessary for the average child to complete a school grade is 164 days, the child who attends the average time of 130.6 days would need ten years in which to complete the same elementary course. In other words, the child loses two years. If, as found in many states, 180 days are necessary, then the child with a school year of 130 days should have eleven years to complete the course.[9]

With the variations that exist in the length of the school year, the number of states not requiring full time attendance, and the irregularity of attendance, there is little in the records of school attendance that warrants our being over optimistic as to present

[8] U. S. Bureau of Education, Bul., 1921-22, No. 31, pp. 2-3.
[9] Table I, Statistical Summary, 1870-1922, U. S. Bureau of Education, Bul., 1921-22, No. 31.

attendance conditions. We can in many instances, however, find some solace in comparing such records for 1920 with those of ten years earlier and see the progress made. As in all social progress we find progress in one area is accompanied by retrogression in another. Not all the states have progressed alike in their solution of the attendance problem. Although the number within the "absolute compulsory" age has made a gain of 4.4 per cent during the 1910-1920 period, we must not lose sight of the fact that 1,438,000 children of that group did not attend school a single day between September 1, 1919, and January 1, 1920.[10]

It must be generally conceded that such figures obtained by the census enumerator would be an under-statement of the total non-attendance. In all probability 3,000,000, or 20 per cent, of the 15,000,000 children over seven and under fourteen years of age were not in regular attendance at any school.

Just as the laws of the states reflect in the main our prevailing conception of the functions of government, so also is their enforcement indicative of the degree in which these conceptions are accepted. That the states are not enforcing the laws has been too clearly revealed.

Like all laws that are not accompanied by adequate means of enforcement the compulsory education law serves largely as an indication of a tendency towards regarding education a little less as a matter of charity and more as a right to be safeguarded by the state. Not yet, however, have all the states reached the point where they are willing to declare for a full public school term.

From an extreme legal minimum of 80 days in Mississippi to the legal maximum of a full term we find varying requirements, such as three fourths of the sessions in Arkansas, one hundred days in Alabama, and four months in South Carolina. It is, however, a general requirement that the school attendance of these shortened terms shall be of consecutive days. Along with such phases of our legal status must be considered the liberal exemption from attendance offered by some states [11] whereby a child, through parental neglect or economic need, might lose almost all of his educational opportunities. In many states these exemp-

---

[10] *Research Bulletin of the N. E. A.,* Vol. IV, Sept. 1923, p. 260.
[11] *Florida School Laws,* 1923, Sec. 286.

tions are disappearing as more far-reaching social legislation begins
to find expression.

For the most part the bibliography of school attendance service offers little of practical assistance to school superintendents
or attendance officers who might be seeking to improve this department of school administration.   Official government bulle-
tins [12] have clearly shown that our theory of compulsory education is far from being worked out in practice.   Educational
leaders in reports and printed articles have constantly called attention to the failure of complete enrollment of the school population, the shortcomings of the school census, and the loss of the
immigrant population, truancy and non-attendance.[13]   The history of compulsory education and child labor [14] has received
scholarly treatment.

Valuable city surveys [15] of recent years have given the results
of more or less careful investigations of city attendance service.
Most of them, however, have devoted a large part of their efforts
to detailed study of administration, finance and adequate building
programs but have given little more than general recommendations for the improvement of attendance service.   The failure of
school administrators to show in their school reports definite evidence of their efforts to enforce the compulsory education laws
and to make available adequate information for true accounting
of their attendance service has resulted in two helpful contributions by which the school authorities may evaluate their system of
records and reports.[16]   More recently several investigations and
studies of a general nature have been made to bring out more
clearly the conditions in the administration of attendance service.

A state-wide study of the cost of compulsory attendance service [17] has been made and suggestions offered as to needed im-
provements in administrative personnel.   It would seem that the

[12] U. S. Bureau of Education, Bul., 1914, No. 2; 1921-22, No. 31; 1922, No. 29;
1917-18, No. 11.
[13] Ayres, L. P., *Child Accounting in the Public Schools.* Cleveland Survey, 1915.
[14] Ensign, F. C., *School Attendance and Child Labor.*
[15] See City Surveys of St. Paul, Minn.; Atlanta, Ga.; Philadelphia, Pa.; Springfield, Mass.; Providence, R. I.; Watertown, N. Y.
[16] Snedden, D. S., and Allen, W. H., *School Reports and School Efficiency.*
    Strayer, G. D. and Engelhardt, N. L., *School Records and Reports.*
[17] Hanson, W. L., *The Cost of Compulsory Attendance Service in the State of New
York and Some Factors Affecting the Cost.*

author of the above-mentioned study had failed to determine the
true census status in some of the cities visited, for there must be
a thorough examination of all records and files in order to have
a full assurance that the actual practice squares with the official
statement of the methods employed. Such a contribution, however, offers new evidence that the attendance service needs re-
organization and adjustment to present standards of efficient school
administration.

The most recent investigation of city school attendance service [18]
has been made by a questionnaire study of 371 cities with populations of 10,000 or over. This study is open to the serious objection that it gives little more than a summary of answers to
questions often misunderstood and occasionally deliberately answered incorrectly. From the number of part-time officers included as source of information and the type of personnel often
found one would expect neither accurate nor fully trustworthy
data. Like so many other studies it merely collects a mass of
information, valuable perhaps, but giving present-day trends
and practices rather than a real program of improvement.

A detailed study of the forms and records used in a large city
for securing school attendance was made in 1913 and a [19] further
adaptation of their uses recommended. It is, however, based
entirely on what was in use in one city rather than on what could
be adopted for extensive service.

The study herein offered was based upon a determined effort
to find out what is actually done in city attendance,—not what is
claimed to be done. Much more time is required to discover
the former than to accept the latter. In each of the fifteen cities
every form used, every file maintained, was examined. Every
objective evidence that could throw any light upon the real situation was sought and detailed notes made. Wherever a continuous
census was claimed the census files were checked with enrollment.
Continuation schools were visited, several thousand transfers,
permanent records and absence reports examined, the data tabulated and actual practice determined. Every form used for census,
regularity of attendance, court action, and child employment was

[18] Bermejo, F. V., *Attendance Service in American Cities.*
[19] Nudd, H. W., *A Description of the Bureau of Compulsory Education of the City of Philadelphia*, 1913.

collected, a detailed description of use was made and the utility of each form for attendance service was investigated.

After the experience gained by this investigation the writer is more strongly convinced than ever that only by such a study can the true status of attendance service be found. A constructive program based upon these findings can then render a real impetus to the betterment of attendance service for cities.

The contribution of this study to attendance service is not so much to point out facts, to show its shortcomings and failures, as to offer constructive suggestions, to show how it can be made more effective and to secure the coöperation of those in the service to work for its increasing betterment.

CHAPTER II

THE ORGANIZATION AND ADMINISTRATION OF ATTENDANCE SERVICE

The increasing compulsory school legislation during the past twenty-five years has thrown new burdens upon the schools. To achieve the results expected and demanded requires an organization whose duty it must be to perform an efficient and adequate attendance service. It is a recognized duty of the school authorities to organize and direct such service and make it fully responsible to them.

No matter what the type of organization may be or how it may actually be administered in practice, its duties and responsibilities shall have three aspects, (*a*) legal or statutory, (*b*) educational, (*c*) social. The laws of the state and the community as to school attendance must be enforced, the educational interests of the child must be safeguarded, and social and economic conditions so often related to the problem of attendance, must not be made an excuse to deprive the child of his rightful schooling.

Before discussing in detail the particular functions of attendance service such as enumeration, regularity of attendance, and child employment it is well to get a general view of the organization and administration as it is found in the fifteen cities of this study. For this purpose the investigation sought to determine the following:

1. The actual type of administrative organization.
2. The relation of the number of officers to the area and population of the city.
3. The adequacy of the clerical staff.
4. The relation of the attendance service to other city agencies.
5. The status of the "Visiting Teacher Movement" in these cities.
6. The physical surroundings under which the attendance service seeks to function.

7. The portion of the attendance officer's time actually spent in different phases of his work.
8. The cost of present attendance service.

Four types of organization are found in the attendance service of cities:

Type 1. Attendance service under the personal direction of the superintendent of schools and responsible to him.

Type 2. Attendance service under the control of the board of education and only indirectly responsible to the superintendent of schools.

Type 3. Attendance service delegated to a person or persons under the general direction, control, and supervision of the superintendent of schools.

Type 4. Attendance service not under the direction of the public school authorities.

Although the first type of organization did not officially prevail in any of the fifteen cities of this study, it is a common type of organization in smaller cities.

Attendance service under Type 2 form of organization is not in accord with principles of school administration, but a marked instance of it is found in City B where there is a noticeable lack of coördination of this department with the superintendent of schools. The attendance department reported directly to and was subject to the control of a committee of the Board of Education. The department feels in no way responsible to the superintendent; a vital relationship between it and the other school divisions is entirely lacking.

The prevailing type of organization, Type 3, is generally accepted in theory and practice in all the cities but one. This type has developed under the necessity for the delegation of responsibility for attendance service in cities where it was realized that the time and energy of the superintendent should be devoted to supervision direction and initiation of administrative policies of his various organizations.

Type 4 has no legal status, but in all the fifteen cities the non-public schools were assuming varying degrees of control over their own attendance service. In City F the public school attendance officer often met the representative of the non-public school investigating the absence of a brother or sister of a child he was investigating. In all other cities the responsibility of the public schools over the attendance of the non-public schools depended upon the possibilities of coöperation and seemed more of a courtesy than an organized responsibility.

Although the authority and responsibility for attendance service had been delegated, no one was charged with the full authority and responsibility for the general control of the department. A divided responsibility prevailed among teachers, principals and attendance officers. Standardization of routine and control of details was noticeably lacking and the regular tabulation of adequate data to check inefficiency was overlooked and neglected in all but Cities A and K.

RELATION OF CITY AREA AND POPULATION TO ATTENDANCE SERVICE

The task of the attendance department is dependent upon the size and population of the city. That these are not always determining factors in the service provided is clearly shown in Table I. We find the range of school enrollment per attendance officer to be from 2,488 pupils to 43,581 pupils. These figures do

TABLE I

COMPARATIVE ATTENDANCE ORGANIZATION STATISTICS

15 SELECTED CITIES [b]

City	Area sq. mi.	Population in 1920 in thousands	School enrollment 1923-24	Average daily attend. 1923-24	No. of attend. off'rs 1923-24	Area of city per att. off. 1923-24	School enroll. per att. officer 1923-24	Average att. per att. off. 1923-24
						Sq. Mi.		
A	49.0	129	24,559	21,119	5[a]	12.2	6,139	5,279
B	18.2	237	43,581	34,818	1	18.2	43,581	34,818
C	8.7	31	6,342	5,232	1	8.7	4,213	5,419
D	8.3	135	25,283	21,132	6[a]	1.6	4,214	3,522
E	3.2	63	13,260	10,843	4[a]	1.08	4,419	3,614
F	5.4	22	5,215	4,506	1	5.42	5,215	4,506
G	5.9	27	5,724	5,724	1	5.9	5,724	5,724
H	1.0	12	3,274	2,385	1	1.0	3,274	2,385
I	10.0	21	4,977	4,090	2	10.0	2,488	2,045
J	4.2	42	15,115	8,600	2	4.2	5,052	4,150
K	71.2	40	55,277	46,572	7	7.9	6,000	5,017
L	21.0	100	20,710	17,896	4	5.2	5,177	4,474
M	38.1	35	8,543	7,859	1	38.1	8,543	7,859
N	10.1	73	15,771	11,595	2	5.66	7,885	5,797
O	17.0	50	10,985	9,353	1	17.0	10,985	9,353

[a] Chief attendance officer who does little or no field work.
[b] Data obtained upon personal visitation.

77104

not include non-public school children for which the attendance department was legally responsible. The laissez-faire attitude towards this part of their task did not make it necessary, in the minds of the school authorities, to base the number of the attendance staff upon total school enrollment.

Only one of the fifteen cities failed to meet the standards set by the *Atlanta Survey.**

It is evident, however, that they have not attained the standards set by the recent action of Philadelphia taken after careful study of the needs of its attendance service. In that city the attendance staff was increased on a basis of one officer for each 4,000 children reported in the school census. This standard recognized the responsibility of the attendance service for all children of compulsory school age whether enrolled in public or enrolled in non-public schools. The appointments were made with the understanding that the ratio will be reduced to one for every 4,000 children in 1925 and one to every 3,500 children in 1926, the contention being that the more nearly they attain the London ratio of 2,500 the more adequately and satisfactorily will they be enabled to handle the absence and behavior problems of school attendance.[1]

In every case, with the exception of City B, there was a complaint of the inability of the department to meet the needs of the schools. Unable to give prompt service to all the cases reported, the departments acknowledged that they were not receiving reports of all illegal absences. This was due to one or all of the following reasons:

1. Lack of confidence in the attendance officer.
2. Limiting names reported to children known to be truants or suspected of truancy.
3. Acceptance of the word of another child for the absence.
4. Known inability of the attendance department to handle all the necessary cases.

* *Atlanta Survey*, Atlanta, Ga., Vol. II, p. 50. "It is a fairly well accepted standard that one attendance officer and one clerk should be provided for each 9,000 to 11,000 pupils, but that the Department will be increased in efficiency and the constructive phases of the service rendered will be increased as this number approaches 6,000."

[1] *Report of Bureau of Compulsory Education*, Philadelphia, 1923, p. 31. Abbott and Breckenridge, *Truancy and Non-Attendance in Chicago*, p. 226. The ratio for London is given as 1,900 children.

5. Acceptances of written excuses and failure to investigate their validity.
6. Limiting reported cases to those absent a specified number of days each month or term.
7. Irregularity of the visits of the attendance officer.

The area of the city and the distance to be traveled by attendance officers has received but little consideration in determining the requirements of the departments. City B, with an area of eighteen square miles and an average of eighty reported cases a day, had the same attendance staff as Cities G and F with five to six square miles of area and an average of twenty reported cases a day. In City F, with an area of five square miles to oversee, the attendance officer found his area so large that he made his investigations on different days in the two sections of the city. The principals of the schools adjusted their absence reports to the section of the city in which they knew the officer would be at work on that day.

There was no apparent realization on the part of school authorities that distance to be traveled lessened the number of cases that could be investigated and that transportation facilities were required for efficient work and for securing the full value of the attendance officer's services. City K, however, had recognized the necessity of determining the amount of service to be rendered by the distance traveled. It had districted the city so that there was an equalization of the attendance officers' burden in terms of children for whom they were responsible and the distance traveled, by allowing the use of a car to the one officer in the more open sections of the city. The attendance department, however, had failed to obtain its request for better transportation facilities in order to increase the general efficiency of all the officers of the city. As the result of a recent school survey City M had just taken action to provide the necessary transportation, thus increasing the efficiency of the attendance staff.

TRAINING OF ATTENDANCE OFFICERS

The number of attendance officers involved in the personal investigation justify no far-reaching conclusions regarding the nation-wide conditions as to previous training of attendance offi-

cers. We can, however, from this study of the training and education of attendance officers in such representative cities, together with the questionnaire studies that have been made, see the
type of occupations that have served as sources for recruiting
the personnel of our attendance service.[2]

TABLE II

PREVIOUS OCCUPATIONS OF ATTENDANCE OFFICERS

15 SELECTED CITIES—1923–24

Previous Occupations	*Number of Officers*
Teachers	4
Saloon-keepers	2
Janitors	2
Social Workers	3
Commercial Training	3
Guards at County Jail	2
Manager of Opera House	1
Professional Baseball Player	1
Policeman	1
Skilled Laborers— Jeweler, Silk Workers, Electrician	5
Clerical	2
College Graduates	4
Housewives	2
Total Reported	32

One third of the officers of these cities are recruited from occupations that would serve as the training for social and child
welfare work which is considered such an important part of
modern attendance service. The previous occupations of the
others may have given them training in those indefinite but highly
desirable factors of "tact" and the "ability to handle people"
which comes from a contact with the world and is not acquired
by school training. It could hardly be said that their previous
occupations gave them the viewpoint or the technique required
for efficient social and welfare work. That the attendance officers
are fully alive to the shortcomings of the present staff and the
need for trained workers in the field is indicated by the resolution
passed at the National Conference of Compulsory Education
Officials held at Springfield, Mass., in October, 1923.[3]

[2] For Attendance Officers in New York State, see Hanson, W. L., *The Cost of Compulsory Attendance in the State of New York*, Table 14.
[3] See *Report of the Bureau of Compulsory Education, Philadelphia, Pa., 1923*, p. 33.

LACK OF CLERICAL HELP

One of the common but serious handicaps under which the attendance service labors is the lack of sufficient clerical assistance. Seven cities or nearly half of the total studied had practically no, or at best very little, clerical assistance. One city with an enrollment of 25,000 pupils and an attendance force of six officers had the assistance of a clerk one half day each week. Under such handicaps it was making some effort to maintain a continuous census. Three cities had no clerical help and the others showed in the breaking down of the records and filing systems a lack of such provisions.

RELATION TO OTHER AGENCIES

The coöperation of attendance departments with other city agencies ranged from pronounced antagonism to full and complete combining of facilities and interests. In City K the department made constant use of the "Social Service Confidential Exchange." In a much smaller city, City G, where the social agencies had been less completely organized, the one attendance officer was a regular attendant at the weekly staff meetings of all recognized social agencies. Duplication of effort had been avoided, unnecessary delays in securing remedial action in cases of poverty had been removed, health and temporary relief and employment had been brought within the effective measures available for the improvement of school attendance.

The Health Department was fully coöperative in all fifteen cities, but the attitude towards the coöperation offered by the police was a matter of indifference, except in those instances where a personal friendship had been formed between members of the two departments. Whatever coöperation existed was apparently based upon personal rather than interdepartmental interest.

THE STATUS OF THE VISITING TEACHER

In three of the cities in our study visiting teachers were employed. In City L the visiting teacher was a regular attendant at the staff meetings of the attendance officers in a more or less advisory capacity and was under the direction of a deputy superintendent who served as Director of Attendance Officers.[4]

[4] For relationship of visiting teacher to attendance department, see Oppenheimer, J. H., *The Visiting Teacher Movement*, p. 195.

In City J the visiting teacher is assigned to the central portion of the city for absence investigations while the official attendance officer takes the outlying areas. Because of the smaller area covered, the visiting teacher is able to give more personal attention to the cases investigated. Special cases from the high school and the foreign section are also referred to her. There is some reason to believe that she is doing a rather polite type of attendance service. The objections from certain sections of the city to visitations from the official attendance officer made a new type necessary and the visiting teacher was the solution. She has charge of court actions and assists in school enumerations. She does some work for the parochial schools but rather as an attendance officer than as a visiting teacher.

The "school visitor" of City I, by virtue of a teacher's certificate, is now recognized as a visiting teacher. She describes her duties as follows:

1. "Secure good attendance in school and improve scholastic record by home investigation, follow up, and personal encouragement to the child."
2. "Take to Children's Court cases that cannot be adjusted by school."
3. "Report to the proper person or organization cases of mental and physical disability."
4. "Prepare employment certificates and coöperate with the continuation school to secure prompt transfer of the child from the day school."
5. "Issue newsboy permits and badges. Secure coöperation of the police and newsdealers in the enforcement of the newsboy laws."
6. "Vocational guidance. Secure positions, when possible, for boys and girls who must leave school."
7. "Social-Betterment-Newsboy Clubs, day classes for foreign-born women, incidental suggestions and assistance in the home, visits to places of employment of children."

From the above it is evident that the visiting teacher's services in these cities are more fully in accord with good attendance service than the accepted ideas of good visiting teacher service. If record keeping constitutes an essential part of the procedure in visiting teacher work, then none of those referred to can be so considered, for there were no "case records" of any kind except the blanks used by the schools for reporting complaints to the visiting teacher.

THE PHYSICAL BACKGROUND OF ATTENDANCE SERVICE

A significant feature of present-day school administration which shows the part attendance service plays in the scheme of education, as visualized by school boards and superintendents of schools, is that physical conditions for attendance service are overlooked and neglected. A brief description of the actual conditions in the cities investigated shows the physical handicaps under which this phase of school administration is working at the present time.

City A.—We find the attendance department in direct connection with the central offices but relegated to the smallest of the suite of rooms. Here four officers and two clerks, with desks taking up nearly all of the available space are compelled to do the work for a school population of 25,000 children. Without privacy of conversation with parents or children on probation, the personal contact necessary in so many of these cases is entirely lost.

City B.—A large office half a mile from the central office has contact by telephone with only 28 out of the 136 schools. The department is out of intimate touch with the disciplinary records, vocational and educational guidance, together with the records of school attendance kept in the central offices. The department is neither physically nor functionally united with the other departments of school administration.

City C.—In a city of over 30,000 the department is largely peripatetic. The attendance records exclusive of the census file and a few other inadequate files were always with the attendance officer or at his home where the record of the work of the day is written up and kept until the annual report requires a brief summary of homes visited and the number of court cases with their dispositions. The officer has no definite assignment of office space.

City D.—A large city attendance department is in the same building with the superintendent of schools but stored away with the municipal janitors and samples of school furniture and supplies in a spacious upper story room. A portion of this room, with low partitions, has been set aside for a city welfare agency. Here the stentorian voice of the "worker" was plainly heard discussing over the phone with the city physician all kinds of venereal diseases while boys and girls were in the attendance office awaiting their working certificates. It would be difficult to imagine a worse condition under which a high-minded officer could seek personal conferences with boys and girls of adolescent age and with mothers and fathers whose children were truants or were seeking employment certificates. The protests of the officer had been in vain.

City E.—The offices were adequate in size but no provisions had been made for special cases requiring individual and personal contact.

City F.—The department was in the same building with the superintendent of schools but located in the basement with the manual training teacher's office and the completed projects of the manual training activities. All conferences, if any, with parents would have to be made standing up if any number were present. Practically no records were kept and the officer kept at hand the tools used by him for school repair work on Saturdays and holidays.

City G.—A well educated, live attendance officer was given an office in the same building with the superintendent of schools but in a room so small that the attendance officer could not confer with more than two persons at a time unless the desk of the part-time clerk were pushed to one side and rendered unavailable for use. Access to the files then became difficult unless those present moved down a narrow corridor towards the door.

City H.—Located fully a mile from the central office, the attendance officer shared her small basement room with the school nurse and dental clinic. Desk room was all that was allotted to the department which was expected to oversee the attendance, registration and employment certificates of a city of 13,000 population. The situation had created the name "three-in-one" departments for the group.

City I.—The attendance department of this city of nearly 25,000 is in a room so inadequate that one of the officers is generally unable to use his desk because of the presence of a supervisor or dental inspector. Three desks with no regular clerical assistance make the office a mere repository for records. With difficulty, conferences with a few boys and girls at a time may be held in the presence of other workers sharing the room.

City J.—A modern city with modern schools, considered well administered, allows its attendance service to attempt to function from a cross corridor near the superintendent's office. The space was large enough for a desk and two chairs, with one occupant being compelled to move aside before the other could go in or come out. The visiting teacher is given desk room in the Board of Education room with others of the clerical and supervisory staff.

City K.—A small office is provided where all the attendance records for a school system of 400,000 must be accessible to the seven attendance officers. As all the employment, census and welfare work is carried on in contiguous offices the conditions are not so trying as in the other cities. There are many evidences, however, in the physical equipment of this part of the school service that attendance is not yet considered a vital, functional force in the efficient administration of the schools.

City L.—A basement supply room with the telephone switchboard operator occupying a part and the census and attendance clerk using the part not taken up by supplies, is the physical expression of the attendance service of this city. In this office centers the service for 20,000 school children.

City M.—A desk in the Board of Education room but close to the office of the superintendent of schools and to the clerical force constitutes the physical equipment of the attendance department. With the force and equipment needed to perform a real service this department would be cramped and unsatisfactory.

City N.—A city of 70,000 with its department in close proximity with the central offices. With one officer in the field most of the time and the other doing office work the office serves well the purpose for which it is used. It would not suffice were the problem of attendance attacked as it should be.

City O.—When a city of 60,000 believes it can satisfactorily perform its attendance service with one man, then the office equipment and office force are usually unimportant items. In this city the superintendent and the attendance service are in constant touch and whatever is needed for the better functioning of the department is made available.

Descriptions from many other cities visited would only increase the number of details and would not show more clearly the place in school administration which the attendance service appears to hold in the minds of those responsible for the organization and administration of the schools. The lack of consideration on the part of school administrators in making adequate physical provision for the attendance service gives indication that regardless of their attitude as expressed in answer to questionnaires or reports, the attendance service is too often incidental, even foreign, to other phases of the administrator's duties and responsibilities.

OFFICERS' TIME REPORTS

City E was the only city investigated that made any attempt to check officers in time spent on the various cases and duties performed. Although these daily reports were supposed to give the actual time spent upon individual cases, the time in schools, and office duties, the reports gave little definite information. In the report of one officer, however, the time distribution was such that an approximate record could be made. A random sampling of 140 daily reports showed that 981 cases had been investigated, or an average of seven each day. Three hundred and fourteen hours or 30 per cent of the officer's time was spent in the schools; 318 hours or 31 per cent in the investigation of cases; 250 hours or 23 per cent in doing clerical work or in the office; the remaining 170 hours or 16 per cent, on a basis of a seven-and-a-half-hour day, was spent in street patrol or in the courts.

Although approximately one-third of the time was spent in office duties and one third in the schools many complaints had been made to the superintendent that the staff was overworked. The three officers were investigating, on an average, twenty-one cases each day, the number considered a fair day's work for one officer in the other cities. No use had been made of these records to reduce the loss of time in visiting schools where for months no absences were reported for investigation. No effort had been made to investigate the time spent in clerical duties.

COST OF ATTENDANCE SERVICE

What a city is willing to pay for its attendance service is one measure of its conception of this responsibility. The cost of this service in the fifteen cities is shown in Table III.

TABLE III

COST OF SCHOOL ATTENDANCE SERVICE [a]
15 CITIES—1923–24

City	School Enrollment	Cost of Attendance Service	Cost per Pupil Enrolled
A	24,559	$15,471.85	.63
B	43,581	11,299.00	.26
C	6,342	1,640.63	.25
D	25,283	12,050.00	.48
E	13,260	9,349.75	.70
F	5,215	1,120.00	.21
G	5,724	2,878.00	.50
H	3,274	1,050.00	.32
I	4,977	3,723.12	.75
J	10,115	5,279.27	.52
K	55,277	24,813.42	.45
L	20,710	6,100.00	.29
M	8,543	2,835.50	.33
N	15,771	3,538.00	.23
O	10,985	3,644.44	.23

[a] Data obtained upon personal visitation.

The per capita cost, based upon the school enrollment, has a range from 21 cents to 70 cents per pupil. All but one had attained the median expenditure per child for enforcement of compulsory education in the cities of New York State, but not one had reached its maximum of 94 cents per child.

There is close agreement between the cost per pupil of attendance service in these cities and the writer's ranking of the efficiency of the service. The character of the service rendered was closely related to the cost per pupil. Not one was offering the complete service that should characterize a city school system. This will be more fully revealed by the further evidence offered.

Our investigations thus far show that:

1. The school superintendents delegate the responsibilities for attendance service but fail to require the records and reports necessary to check the efficiency of the service.

2. The public school attendance service is incomplete and often lacking entirely for non-public schools.

3. The previous training and educational qualifications of attendance officers are not adequate for the type of service now being demanded.

4. A large part of the control of illegal absence investigation is with the individual school because of the inability of the attendance department to investigate all cases.

5. Little if any consideration is given to the area of the city in determining the number of attendance officers or the provisions for necessary transportation.

6. The public school enrollment and not the total school enrollment is considered the measure of the attendance officer's responsibilities.

7. A significant feature of present-day attendance service is the neglect of the importance of physical equipment and surroundings in the efficient administration of the department.

8. The more recent employees are men and women of better educational preparation than the older type of attendance officer. One city requires written examinations for appointments to the attendance service and five college graduates are employed.

9. In service training for a more scientific approach to the problems of attendance service is offered in two cities.

10. The clerical assistance is insufficient and often entirely lacking.

11. The generally accepted functions of the "visiting teacher" is largely lost sight of in her regular attendance duties.

12. The attendance service is not fully coöperative with other community welfare agencies.

CHAPTER III

REGISTRATION OF SCHOOL POPULATION

The accurate enumeration of the school population has three outstanding purposes: (a) as a basis upon which the school authorities, both state and local, may determine the effectiveness of the enforcement of the compulsory education law, (b) to secure state revenue on the basis of the total school population to be legally enumerated, (c) to provide the optimum educational service for all children for whom the state and the community feel an educational responsibility.

For these purposes the school authorities must be provided with such adequate information that they may determine: *

1. How many children live within the jurisdiction of the school authorities.
2. Where these children live.
3. Who is responsible for these children.
4. On what date these children are of compulsory school age.
5. How many ought to be in school.
6. How many are in public schools.
7. How many are in non-public schools.
8. How many are not in school at all, and why.
9. What special provisions should be made.

The next problem in our investigation was to determine (a) the actual status of the school census, (b) the extent to which the census was checked for its accuracy with other enumerations and the school enrollment, (c) the cost of school census as found in the reports of fifty cities and in the cities studied, (d) the type of school census, if any, actually in force in the cities studied and (e) the objectives of a school census, and (f) how these objectives could be attained.

* See Habens, Paul B., "The Factors of an Adequate School Census." *Journal of the National Educational Association,* Vol. I, No. 10. June, 1917, p. 1063.

PRESENT STATUS OF SCHOOL CENSUS

All but three states require or permit a school census,[1] but the testimony of educators has long called our attention to the failures in the present American practice.[2]

The present status of the school census as disclosed by a recent study was expressed in these words: "It was hoped that facts of importance could be worked out from the relations between school census figures and public school enrollment, but of all the cities participating only one third were able to give school census data by ages. That so few school systems are now organized to take such a census and keep it up to date is one of the outstanding features of this survey."[3]

From the unpublished data of this inquiry we were able to make, in Table IV, a distribution by ages of all the reporting cities with a population of over 20,000. From such tabulation we discover the wide variations in the total age-spans, as well as other important factors of a school census, used by the cities reporting. Only fifteen out of fifty-four cities take a school census of their four-year-old children. Thirteen start with the five-year-old children, while all but one included the children who were six years old. The limits of the compulsory school years caused eight to omit all beyond fifteen years of age and only twenty cities included all the population from the time the children had reached the age of six and should be in school, until they had reached majority.

In the study of the annual reports of 1923–24 of fifty cities, fifteen gave no information regarding the total school enumeration, and this information was given in twenty-four different age-groups, thirteen giving the data by years. Such a diversity of age-spans and the fact that "twenty-seven different age-spans have been utilized since 1900 in securing school census data in various cities of the United States"[4] show the need for more adequate and uniform school census records.

We find more than twenty instances in the first ten cities where the even years have a larger population than the odd years. This

[1] U. S. Bureau of Education, Bulletin No. 11, 1918, p. 78.
[2] Ayres, L. P., *Laggards in Our Schools*, p. 191.
[3] McGaughy, J. R., *Know and Help Your Schools, Second Report*, p. 17.
[4] Strayer, G. D. and Engelhardt, N. L., *The Class-Room Teacher*, p. 277.

TABLE

SCHOOL CENSUS

54 CITIES

No.	Cities	4 yrs.	5 yrs.	6 yrs.	7 yrs.	8 yrs.	9 yrs.
1.	Cleveland, O.	....	....	20,509	18,709	18,226	17,441
2.	St. Louis, Mo.	....	....	12,077	11,873	12,173	11,883
3.	Pittsburgh, Pa.	....	....	12,088	12,243	12,001	11,685
4.	Milwaukee, Wis.	12,070	10,412	10,063	....	8,840	8,744
5.	New Orleans, La.	....	....	10,452	7,773	7,762	7,186
6.	Seattle, Wash.	4,174	4,695	4,787	4,749	4,721	4,366
7.	Denver, Colo.	....	....	4,949	4,444	4,645	4,614
8.	Providence, R. I.	....	4,688	4,775	4,637	4,501	4,469
9.	Columbus, O.	....	....	3,206	3,206	3,327	3,447
10.	Akron, O.	....	....	3,544	3,283	3,105	2,964
11.	Birmingham, Ala.	....	....	4,782	4,496	4,755	4,347
12.	Richmond, Va.	....	....	2,828	3,639	3,308	3,157
13.	New Haven, Conn.	2,999	3,701	3,333	3,385	3,204	3,167
14.	Grand Rapids, Mich.	2,678	2,816	2,833	2,720	2,720	2,549
15.	Fall River, Mass.	....	2,336	2,455	2,442	2,512	2,430
16.	Lowell, Mass.	....	1,058	1,556	1,448	1,544	2,138
17.	Reading, Pa.	275	494	605	697	1,638	1,710
18.	Tacoma, Wash.	1,334	1,603	1,666	1,675	1,715	1,614
19.	Elizabeth, N. J.	2,222	2,154	2,063	1,820	1,986	1,792
20.	Somerville, Mass.	....	1,079	1,445	1,625	1,656	1,507
21.	Schenectady, N. Y.	253	1,389	2,139	1,918	1,984	1,830
22.	Savannah, Ga.	....	....	1,534	1,494	1,462	1,446
23.	Troy, N. Y.	768	802	809	808	828	877
24.	Terre Haute, Ind.	....	....	1,057	1,066	1,146	1,101
25.	Saginaw, Mich.	....	620	741	854	790	804
26.	Altoona, Pa.	....	....	1,170	1,149	1,184	1,139
27.	Mobile, Ala.	....	....	1,224	1,061	1,113	1,019
28.	Roanoke, Va.	....	....	1,005	1,067	1,061	984
29.	Winston-Salem, N. C.	....	....	751	755	772	735
30.	Bay City, Mich.	....	1,274	1,291	1,342	1,367	1,231
31.	York, Pa.	....	....	758	845	783	831
32.	Cedar Rapids, Ia.	....	1,290	833	835	754	838
33.	Elmira, N. Y.	203	394	329	614	656	682
34.	Newcastle, Pa.	....	....	722	767	882	899
35.	Woonsocket, R. I.	....	177	343	412	396	376
36.	Chelsea, Mass.	....	1,174	1,195	1,046	1,017	1,065
37.	Kenosha, Wis.	735	931	919	870	813	833
38.	Everett, Mass.	....	614	771	801	835	775
39.	Wichita Falls, Tex.	....	....	....	637	665	595
40.	Springfield, Mo.	....	....	782	720	826	747
41.	Madison, Wis.	614	690	607	696	627	600
42.	Lorain, O.	....	....	973	973	920	850
43.	Muskegon, Mich.	....	634	673	704	672	643
44.	Muncie, Ind.	....	....	825	710	694	760
45.	Battle Creek, Mich.	....	514	675	592	576	557
46.	Portsmouth, O.	....	....	726	703	622	616
47.	Watertown, N. Y.	363	781	640	530	571	557
48.	Sheboygan, Wis.	776	716	748	544	639	528
49.	Newport, R. I.	....	225	289	342	318	322
50.	Colorado Springs, Colo.	....	....	516	520	587	557
51.	Zanesville, O.	....	....	519	459	517	426
52.	Phœnix, Ariz.	....	....	911	784	790	716
53.	Richmond, Ind.	....	....	413	441	432	416
54.	Norwich, Conn.	200	354	394	331	338	346

error, so common in census taking, would be avoided were the legal evidences of age required in taking the census. Those uncertain as to their age will give an even number when questioned about their ages more often than they will give an odd number.[5]

It is highly improbable that there could be no change in the

[5] Ayres, L. P., *Child Accounting in the Public Schools*, p. 20.

IV

DISTRIBUTION BY AGES

1920

10 yrs.	11 yrs.	12 yrs.	13 yrs.	14 yrs.	15 yrs.	16 yrs.	17 yrs.	18 yrs.	19 yrs.	20 yrs.
17,600	15,905	17,031	14,931	14,008	11,677	12,631	11,955	12,698	11,501	13,633
12,164	11,922	12,417	11,084	10,786	9,748	10,869	9,592	9,529	13,593	....
12,015	10,896	10,873	10,222	19,957	9,362	....	....	....	....	....
8,557	8,288	7,754	8,198	7,556	7,089	6,615	6,368	6,467	6,367	7,473
7,641	6,981	7,573	7,254	7,135	6,266	5,964	5,460	5,011	....	....
4,317	4,213	4,192	4,014	3,818	3,543	3,508	3,459	3,342	2,879	2,520
4,641	4,343	4,577	4,109	4,210	3,357	3,665	3,206	3,254	3,152	3,078
4,312	4,254	4,354	4,033	3,948	3,697	3,457	....	....	....	....
3,447	3,447	3,447	3,447	3,170	2,898	2,588	2,282	2,082	....	....
2,847	2,629	2,743	2,530	2,262	2,634	2,080	2,071	2,509	2,241	1,919
4,724	4,051	4,771	3,876	3,568	3,405	3,293	2,773	2,767	2,197	2,010
3,181	2,982	3,041	2,759	2,763	2,511	2,799	2,669	2,844	2,366	....
2,958	2,826	2,958	2,844	2,551	2,547	....	....	....	....	....
2,527	2,454	2,575	2,400	2,357	2,275	2,232	2,226	2,172	2,313	....
2,394	2,461	2,387	2,236	1,710	1,562	1,506	....	....	....	....
1,928	2,280	2,236	1,710	1,562	1,506	....	....	....	....	....
1,763	1,724	1,735	1,741	1,692	1,106	660	....	....	....	....
1,599	1,546	1,500	1,539	1,530	1,397	1,370	1,310	1,250	1,091	996
1,845	1,705	1,603	1,496	1,414	1,190	1,374	1,130	1,016	....	....
1,611	1,546	1,541	1,554	1,149	991	....	....	....	....	....
1,720	1,653	1,786	1,477	1,676	1,345	1,389	1,256	....	....	....
1,439	1,281	1,258	1,233	1,171	928	857	755	....	....	....
808	767	852	816	755	676	702	604	....	....	....
1,136	1,121	1,170	1,152	1,195	1,033	1,164	1,060	1,127	907	747
804	760	777	721	750	675	709	694	710	537	....
1,079	1,121	1,167	1,114	1,006	1,104	....	....	....	....	....
1,059	1,033	1,079	1,041	973	853	897	757	758	625	376
1,041	972	994	845	886	774	734	778	780	638	....
749	676	753	640	735	670	779	771	821	695	630
1,187	1,173	838	754	807	741	677	531	502	404	....
764	818	796	781	829	820	....	....	....	....	....
750	781	803	764	818	736	869	816	819	972	1,226
600	704	671	605	636	590	567	562	527	378	180
779	749	825	796	648	460	274	209	96	32	12
410	409	515	538	357	128	74	63	....	....	..
1,001	1,012	917	897	823	855	....	....	....	....	..
746	684	696	675	606	555	478	474	435	439	..
796	777	792	734	657	718	....	....	....	....	..
572	542	525	517	488	467	391	376	....	....	..
784	753	822	761	725	629	662	573	547	435	..
619	562	601	566	551	491	556	530	437	417	..
815	770	740	683	600	559	450	445	420	410	400
644	575	611	574	587	542	548	545	576	527	....
740	756	692	525	465	460	426	410	409	482	513
590	544	564	557	544	539	523	544	505	452	....
594	592	570	570	566	545	555	528	525	522	520
557	545	616	584	556	561	530	540	517	536	523
572	572	626	541	542	425	457	487	447	385	....
347	331	342	307	308	276	207	108	....	....	....
483	578	524	561	526	567	592	534	628	455	431
480	419	471	439	450	410	402	450	416	285	225
700	711	731	636	677	563	606	535	488	419	419
400	398	431	402	398	378	394	359	312	277	249
314	339	332	250	105	36	7	3	....	....	....

population for five different age-groups as in Columbus, Ohio, or that there could be such a rapid falling off in the population between the fifteen-year-olds and the sixteen-year-olds as in Reading, Pa. Many other cases of apparent inaccuracies and variations from any recognized population distributions are easily pointed out.

TABLE V

The Per Cent Each Year of the 1920 School Census Is of the Total 1920 Federal Census 54 Cities Reporting to Educational Finance Inquiry

No.	Population 1920	% 4 yr.	% 5 yr.	% 6 yr.	% 7 yr.	% 8 yr.	% 9 yr.	% 10 yr.	% 11 yr.	% 12 yr.	% 13 yr.	% 14 yr.	% 15 yr.	% 16 yr.	% 17 yr.	% 18 yr.	% 19 yr.	% 20 yr.
1	796,836	....	....	2.57	2.35	2.27	2.18	2.21	2.00	2.13	1.87	1.75	1.46	1.58	1.50	1.59	1.44	1.71
2	772,897	....	....	1.56	1.53	1.57	1.53	1.57	1.54	1.60	1.43	1.39	1.26	1.40	1.24	1.23	1.75	....
3	588,193	....	....	2.05	2.08	2.04	1.98	2.04	1.85	1.85	1.73	1.69	1.59	1.39	....	1.39	1.63	....
4	457,147	2.64	2.27	2.20	1.93	1.91	1.87	1.81	1.69	1.79	1.65	1.55	1.44	1.54	1.41	1.29	....	....
5	387,219	....	....	2.69	2.00	2.00	1.85	1.97	1.80	1.95	1.87	1.84	1.61	1.11	1.41	1.05	.91	.79
6	315,652	1.32	1.48	1.51	1.50	1.49	1.39	1.81	1.34	1.32	1.27	1.21	1.12	1.42	1.09	1.26	1.23	1.20
7	256,369	....	....	1.92	1.73	1.81	1.88	1.81	1.69	1.79	1.63	1.64	1.37	1.45	1.25	....	....	....
8	237,595	....	1.97	2.00	1.95	1.89	1.88	1.81	1.79	1.83	1.69	1.66	1.55	1.09	.96	.96	.87	....
9	237,031	....	....	1.35	1.35	1.40	1.45	1.45	1.26	1.45	1.20	1.33	1.22	.99	.99	1.24	1.07	.87
10	208,435	....	....	1.69	1.57	1.48	1.41	1.36	1.45	1.31	1.45	1.08	.97	1.84	.96	1.07	1.23	.90
11	178,270	....	....	2.68	2.52	2.66	2.43	2.64	2.27	2.67	2.17	2.00	1.91	1.63	1.55	1.55	1.37	1.12
12	171,667	....	....	2.52	2.11	1.92	1.83	1.85	1.73	1.77	1.60	1.60	1.46	....	1.55	1.65	1.23	....
13	162,519	1.84	2.28	1.64	2.08	1.97	1.95	1.82	1.78	1.82	1.75	1.56	1.56	1.62	1.61	1.67	1.37	1.02
14	137,634	1.94	2.04	2.05	1.97	1.97	1.83	1.83	1.78	1.86	1.74	1.72	1.65	....	....	....	....	....
15	120,485	....	1.93	2.06	2.02	2.08	2.01	1.98	2.04	1.98	2.00	1.93	1.78	.61	.61	....	1.68	....
16	112,759	.25	.93	1.37	1.28	1.36	1.89	1.71	2.23	1.98	1.51	1.38	1.26	1.41	....	1.28	....	....
17	107,784	1.37	.45	.56	.65	1.51	1.68	1.63	1.60	1.61	1.61	1.57	1.44	1.43	1.35	1.06	1.28	1.12
18	96,965	2.32	1.65	1.71	1.72	1.76	1.66	1.64	1.59	1.54	1.58	1.57	1.26	1.24	1.18	....	1.06	1.13
19	95,682	....	2.25	2.15	1.89	2.07	1.87	1.92	1.78	1.67	1.56	1.47	1.06	1.06	1.41	....	....	....
20	93,091	.39	1.15	1.55	1.74	2.77	1.61	1.73	1.66	1.65	1.07	1.23	1.51	1.56	.90	1.70	....	....
21	88,723	....	1.56	2.41	2.16	2.23	2.06	1.94	1.86	2.01	1.66	1.88	1.11	1.02	.83	1.14	1.37	1.37
22	83,252	1.06	....	1.84	1.79	1.75	1.73	1.72	1.53	1.50	1.47	1.40	1.02	.97	.90	....	.86	....
23	72,013	....	1.11	1.12	1.12	1.14	1.21	1.12	1.06	1.18	1.13	1.13	.93	1.14	....	1.26	....	1.37
24	66,083	....	....	1.59	1.61	1.73	1.66	1.71	1.69	1.77	1.74	1.80	1.56	1.49	1.12	1.53	.86	.86
25	61,903	....	1.00	1.19	1.37	1.27	1.29	1.29	1.23	1.25	1.76	1.21	1.09	1.44	....	1.69	....	....
26	60,331	....	....	1.94	1.90	1.96	1.88	1.78	1.85	1.93	1.84	1.66	1.82	1.60	1.25	1.05	....	.62
27	60,151	....	....	2.03	1.76	1.85	1.69	1.76	1.71	1.79	1.73	1.61	1.41	1.49	1.25	1.26	1.03	....
28	50,842	....	....	1.97	2.09	2.08	1.93	2.04	1.91	1.95	1.66	1.74	1.52	1.44	1.53	1.53	1.25	1.30
29	48,395	2.67	1.55	1.55	1.56	1.59	1.51	1.54	1.39	1.55	1.32	1.51	1.38	1.60	1.59	1.69	1.43	....
30	47,554	....	2.67	2.71	2.82	2.87	2.58	2.49	2.46	1.76	1.58	1.69	1.55	1.42	1.11	1.05	.84	....
31	47,512	....	1.59	1.59	1.77	1.64	1.74	1.60	1.71	1.67	1.58	1.74	1.72	1.72	1.79	1.79	....	....
32	45,566	....	1.82	1.82	1.83	1.65	1.83	1.64	1.55	1.76	1.67	1.79	1.61	1.90	1.24	1.16	2.13	2.69
33	45,305	.44	2.83	.72	1.35	1.44	1.50	1.32	1.66	1.48	1.33	1.40	1.30	1.25	.46	.21	.83	.39
34	44,938	....	.86	1.60	1.70	1.96	2.00	1.73	.94	1.83	1.77	1.44	1.02	.60	.14	....	.07	.02
35	43,496	....	.40	.78	.94	.91	.86	.94	....	1.18	1.23	.82	.29	.17	....	....	....	....
36	43,184	....	2.71	2.76	2.42	2.35	2.46	2.31	2.34	2.12	2.07	1.91	1.97	....	....	....	....	....

	No. of cases																
37	40,472	1.81	2.30	2.27	2.14	2.00	2.05	1.84	1.69	1.71	1.66	1.49	1.37	1.18	1.17	1.07	1.08	·
38	40,120	·	1.53	1.92	1.99	2.08	1.93	1.98	1.93	1.97	1.82	1.63	1.78	·	·	·	·	·
39	40,079	·	·	1.97	1.59	1.66	1.48	1.42	1.35	1.30	1.28	1.21	1.16	.97	.93	1.38	1.09	·
40	39,631	1.59	1.79	1.58	1.81	2.08	1.88	1.97	1.90	2.07	1.92	1.82	1.58	1.67	1.44	1.13	1.08	·
41	38,378	·	·	2.60	2.60	2.46	2.27	1.61	1.46	1.98	1.47	1.43	1.27	1.44	1.38	1.12	1.13	·
42	37,295	·	1.73	1.84	1.93	1.83	1.75	2.18	2.06	1.67	1.83	1.60	1.49	1.20	1.19	1.57	1.44	1.07
43	36,570	·	·	2.25	1.94	1.90	2.08	1.76	1.57	1.89	1.56	1.60	1.48	1.49	1.12	1.19	1.31	1.40
44	36,524	·	1.49	1.81	1.63	1.59	1.54	2.02	2.06	1.55	1.44	1.27	1.25	1.16	·	1.39	1.24	1.57
45	35,164	·	·	2.19	2.12	1.88	1.86	1.63	1.50	1.72	1.54	1.50	1.49	1.44	1.50	1.59	1.58	1.67
46	33,011	1.16	2.49	2.04	1.69	1.82	1.78	1.79	1.79	1.96	1.72	1.72	1.65	1.68	1.59	1.65	1.71	·
47	31,285	·	2.31	2.09	1.75	2.06	1.88	1.78	1.74	2.02	1.86	1.77	1.79	1.69	1.72	1.44	1.24	·
48	30,955	2.50	.74	.95	1.13	1.05	1.06	1.84	1.84	1.13	1.74	1.75	1.37	1.47	1.57	·	·	·
49	30,255	·	·	1.71	1.72	1.94	1.85	1.14	1.09	1.74	1.01	1.01	.91	.68	.35	2.08	1.51	1.43
50	30,105	·	·	1.75	1.55	1.74	1.44	1.60	1.92	1.59	1.86	1.74	1.88	1.96	1.77	1.40	.96	.75
51	29,559	·	·	3.13	2.69	2.71	2.46	1.62	1.41	2.51	1.48	1.52	1.38	1.35	1.52	1.67	1.44	1.44
52	29,053	·	·	1.54	1.64	1.61	1.55	2.40	2.44	1.61	2.18	2.33	1.93	2.08	1.84	1.16	1.03	.93
53	29,000	·	·	·	·	·	·	1.49	1.48	·	1.50	1.48	1.41	1.47	1.34	·	·	·
54	22,304	.89	1.58	1.76	1.48	1.51	1.55	1.40	1.52	1.48	1.12	·	·	·	·	·	·	·
Number of cases		15	28	53	54	54	54	54	54	54	54	53	53	44	42	36	34	20
Total percent		21.52	47.50	98.35	97.37	98.90	95.81	94.54	92.18	93.76	86.97	82.68	75.26	59.76	53.98	48.59	41.95	23.15
		1.44	1.70	1.86	1.80	1.83	1.77	1.75	1.71	1.74	1.16	1.56	1.42	1.36	1.28	1.35	1.23	1.16

As these returns were for the same year as the Federal Census it is possible to study any cities or group of cities and compare the school census with the federal census of the same age.

In Table VI, below, we have made such a comparison of all the cities with the age-span six years to twenty years inclusive.[6]

Ayres in his study of the accuracy of the school census states [7] that the "proportion of people in the population who are from six

TABLE VI
School Census Distribution—20 Cities

No.	City	Population in 1920[a]	Total Per Cent 6–20 yrs.	6–20 yrs. of School Census	6–20 yrs. Incl. Federal Census
1.	Cleveland, O.	796,836	28.61	227,975	201,195
2.	Seattle, Wash.	315,652	18.46	58,269	65,550
3.	Denver, Colo.	256,369	23.54	60,349	56,097
4.	Akron, O.	208,435	18.52	38,602	46,361
5.	Birmingham, Ala.	178,270	31.24	55,692	50,821
6.	Tacoma, Wash.	96,965	22.39	21,710	22,891
7.	Terre Haute, Ind.	66,083	24.42	16,137	17,181
8.	Mobile, Ala.	60,151	22.99	13,829	16,590
9.	Winston-Salem, N. C.	48,359	22.51	10,894	15,124
10.	Cedar Rapids, Ia.	45,466	27.61	12,581	11,205
11.	Elmira, N. Y.	45,305	18.26	8,273	10,510
12.	Newcastle, Pa.	44,938	18.07	8,120	12,235
13.	Lorain, O.	37,295	26.78	9,988	10,395
14.	Muncie, Ind.	36,524	24.28	8,868	9,578
15.	Portsmouth, Ind.	33,011	26.45	8,731	8,882
16.	Watertown, N. Y.	31,285	26.67	8,344	7,380
17.	Colorado Springs, Colo.	30,105	26.71	8,041	7,266
18.	Zanesville, O.	29,569	21.46	6,346	7,984
19.	Phoenix, Ariz.	29,053	33.25	9,660	6,997
20.	Richmond, Ind.	26,765	21.24	5,685	6,347

[a] Data obtained from 1920 Census, Vol. III.

to twenty years of age is about 27 per cent of the entire population" and that "the ratio of children of these school ages to the entire population is a nearly constant ratio in cities of a similar sort."

The returns given by the twenty cities for the group when compared with the Federal Census show that in only eight cities did the school census meet or approximate that ratio. In fact the range was from 18.07 to 33.25 per cent.

[6] The method used in obtaining the number of six-year-old children from the Federal Census was that of the Finance Inquiry, Teachers College, Columbia University, New York.

[7] Ayres, L. P., *Child Accounting in the Public Schools*, p. 13.

Using data found in Table V and age distribution in per cent as found in the Federal Census for that year we see in Table VII the wide variation between the Federal and School Census.

By omitting such obvious inaccuracies as the last four years of Norwich, Conn., and Woonsocket, R. I., we can find the central tendency of the different age-groups which should indicate an approximate measure of these age-groups as determined by a school census.

TABLE VII

COMPARISON BETWEEN AVERAGE PER CENT OF TOTAL POPULATION OF SCHOOL CENSUS BY AGES AND THE FEDERAL CENSUS DISTRIBUTION

54 CITIES—1920

Ages	*4*	*5*	*6*	*7*	*8*	*9*	*10*	*11*	*12*
U. S. (Census 1920)...	2.2	2.2	2.2	2.2	2.2	2.0	2.1	2.0	2.1
Average for 54 Cities..	1.4	1.7	1.86	1.8	1.83	1.77	1.75	1.71	1.74
Difference in Per Cent	.8	.5	.34	.4	.37	.23	.35	.29	.39

Ages	*13*	*14*	*15*	*16*	*17*	*18*	*19*	*20*
U. S. (Census 1920).......	1.9	1.9	1.8	1.9	1.8	1.8	1.7	1.7
Average for 54 cities [a]......	1.16	1.56	1.42	1.36	1.28	1.35	1.23	1.16
Difference in Per Cent......	.74	.34	.38	.54	.52	.45	.47	.54

[a] Reprint, 14th Federal Census, Vol. II, Chap. III, Table II, p. 168.

CHECKING SCHOOL CENSUS

From the reports of forty cities in answer to the question, "Is the census checked with the public school enrollment?" twenty-seven cities reported "yes," one answered "will be" and eleven answered "no." One answered "no, but hope to." [8]

That these reports only mention public school enrollment would indicate that checking the census with total school enrollment, public and non-public, is not considered necessary.

In the annual reports, 1923–24, of fifty cities, three compared the school census with the Federal Census, nine discussed the importance of the census and nine gave age-group data regarding the non-public schools. In only seventeen items did five or more cities give comparable data. These included such facts as the number of deaf and dumb, the cost of enumeration, age-groups 5–7, 6–21,

[8] U. S. Bureau of Education, City Leaflet, No. 3, p. 26.

7–14 years, total enumeration and the number not attending. In no item, other than total enumeration, did more than twelve cities give any data.

COST OF SCHOOL CENSUS

Out of fifty annual city reports for 1923–24, only twelve gave the cost of the census department. The lack of such data in the reports is but another evidence of the lack of importance of the enumeration of the school population as the school administrators often view it. School enrollments, already large and in many instances overcrowded, arouse little enthusiasm for a gleaning of the strays that might be overlooked.

TABLE VIII

COST OF THE CENSUS AS GIVEN IN 12 ANNUAL CITY REPORTS

1923–1924

City	Enrollment	Cost of Census	Cost per Pupil Enrolled
Allentown, Pa.	15,771	$452.70	.028
Bristol, Conn.	5,055	153.88	.03
Cedar Rapids, Ia.	24,930	8,166.00	.327
Columbus, O.	38,187	2,057.00	.053
Dayton, O.	26,102	1,562.34	.059
Moline, Ill.	3,879	217.00	.056
New Haven, Conn.	32,067	2,029.40	.063
Northampton, Mass.	3,429	203.00	.059
Portland, Me.	11,719	1,095.00	.093
Williamsport, Pa.	5,674	366.75	.065
Bethlehem, Pa.	10,985	564.44	.051
Cincinnati, O.	54,202	6,280.00	.115
Average			.083 [a]

[a] U. S. Bureau of Education, City School Leaflet, No. 3, Oct. 1922. Range from two cents to twenty cents per pupil in 31 cities.

That cities should range in per pupil census cost from approximately three cents to thirty-two cents shows a wide variation in possible educational service. Of the cities studied the census of City N cost three cents per pupil. The census was taken to meet state requirements for age-groups and was not actually available for any real help in the enforcement of the compulsory education law until nine months later. City A showed a cost of seven cents per pupil and was the most accurate continuing registration of the school population, both public and private, that was found. The chief attendance officer estimated that the constant enumeration required to make the census continuing would bring the cost up to 16 cents per pupil.

City K had made a most complete annual census at an expense of eleven cents per pupil, but made very few if any corrections during the year. If City A had been able to have the accurate enumeration of City K, it would then have had available a most accurate and complete knowledge of its school population. As none of the cities visited had a continuing census of the total school population, it is impossible to give a more accurate estimate than the one mentioned above, which is considered a fair per pupil cost for a continuing census.

SUMMARY OF THE CENSUS STATUS IN 15 SELECTED CITIES

By a detailed investigation of the methods employed in the taking of the school census in these cities it was possible to discover many divergencies between theory and practice and between the type of census legally required and the type actually in force.

Two methods for determining the school population are recognized: (1) a census or enumeration based upon a state law and taken annually or at irregular yearly intervals, and (2) a continuing census or enumeration which is maintained in such a way that at any time one would be able to obtain from the records in the central office accurate, complete and up-to-date information regarding how many children live within the district, their age, grade, school and other information considered necessary for the educational program of the community, the enforcement of the compulsory education law and the child labor laws.

Table IX gives a summary showing the actual status of the school census in the fifteen cities investigated. These cities may be considered in three groups:

> Group I: Cities B, K, M, N, O—annual census.
> Group II: Cities A, C, D, I, J, L—continuing census.
> Group III: Cities E, F, G, H—no census.

The cities in Group I were required by state law to take an annual census.

From a detailed examination of the census in City B it was evident that the underlying spirit was financial rather than educational. The enumerator checked the list of those names previously obtained through school and factory. After the results were tabulated the census clerks were dismissed until the next census.

In City M the enumeration sheets were found to be on legal cap paper and put away without further use after the required state report had been made. In City N there was a serious lack of system in the house-to-house canvass. The enumerators had often begun the enumeration at any point in the block and had taken the census to the next corner, then down a side street or an alley. As a result the names of residents in the same block were found interspersed with residents of other blocks. Only verbal instructions had been given to the enumerators.

In City O a continuing census was claimed. The investigation, however, disclosed that an annual census had been taken of the children six to sixteen years of age, the state report rendered and the census books tied in bundles and filed. The enumeration period lasted from April to September in order to allow the teachers and principals an opportunity to attend summer school and take the census "in odd moments." Typed lists of the 2,300 non-public school pupils or seventeen per cent of the total school population are received once each year.

The cities in this group, with the exception of City K, had met the legal requirements for the census in so far as it was necessary to obtain information for the state report. The methods of enumeration were careless, inefficient, and showed no desire to make a complete accounting of the school population.

The cities of Group II claimed a continuing census but only in Cities A and J was there an acknowledged endeavor to maintain other than a registration of the children actually enrolled in the public schools. Not one of the cities of this group had had an enumeration since 1919, although City J does attempt from school reports to discover children who are non-attendants and should be enrolled. As the non-public schools offer little cooperation the census is acknowledged as incomplete for the total school population.

City A had an accurate registration of all public school children and made serious effort to keep it accurate. By semiannual inquiries from all pupils in the city the teachers obtain the names of any children between five and sixteen years who are not at-

TABLE IX
Census Organization and Administration
15 Selected Cities. Data Obtained Upon Visitation

	Cities															
	A	B	C	D	E	F	G	H	I	J	K	L	M	N	O
1. Type of census (A—Annual; C—Continuous)	C	A	C	C					C	C	A	C	A	A	A
2. Date of last enumeration		'24	'17	'19					'17	'19	'24	'19	'24	'24	'24
3. By whom taken (E—App. Enum.; T—Teachers; P—Principals)	E	E	T	E					E	E	E	E	T	P	T
4. When taken	M	J	M	S					M	M	M	M	S	Je	A-S
5. Checked for reliability (Y—Yes; N—No)	Y	Y	N	N					N	Y	Y	N	Y	N	N
a. Federal census	N	N	N	N					N	N	N	N	N	N	N
b. School enroll.	Y	Y	Y	N					N	Y	Y	N	Y	N	N
c. House file	N	N	N	N					N	N	N	N	N	N	N
6. Maps or records showing city growth	Y	Y	N	N					N	N	Y	N	N	N	N
7. Tabulation of census—															
a. Age groups	Y	Y	Y						Y	Y	Y	Y	Y	Y	Y
b. Grades	N	Y							N	N	Y		N	N	N
c. Schools—															
Private	Y	Y	Y						N		Y		N	N	N
Parochial	Y	Y	Y						N		Y	X	N	N	N
Public	Y	Y	Y						N		Y	X	N	N	N
d. Nationalities	N	N	N						N		Y	N	N	N	N
e. Occupations	N	N	N						N		Y	N	N	N	N
f. Not attending	Y	Y	N	N					N	N	Y	N	N	N	N
8. Type of enumeration	2	1	2						2	2	3	2	2	2	2
9. By whom revised (A—Att. Dept.; S—Supt. Office)	A		S	A					A	S		A			
10. Methods of revision—															
a. Change of residence	Y	N	Y	Y					N	Y	N	N	N	N	N
b. New residents	Y	N	Y	Y					Y	Y	N	N	N	N	N
c. New residences	Y	N	Y	N					N	Y	N	N	N	N	N
d. Houses vacated	N	N	N	N					N	N	N	N	N	N	N
11. Frequency of revision (A—Annual; I—Incomplete; W—Weekly; M—Monthly; D—Daily)	D	A	I	I					M	W	A		A	A	A
12. School reports—															
a. Frequency	DW	N	W	M			W		M	W	N	M	M	N	M
b. Admissions	Y	N	Y	Y			X		Y	Y	N	X	X	N	X
c. Changes of address	Y	N	Y	Y			X		Y	Y	N	X	X	N	X
d. Transfers	Y	N	Y	Y			X		Y	Y	N	X	X	N	X
e. Discharges (X—School registration, not actual census)	Y	N	Y	Y			X		Y	Y	N	X	X	N	X
13. Reports of enumerators	N	N	N	N					N	N	N	N	N	N	N
School reports—															
a. Public	Y	N	Y	Y			Y		Y	Y	N	Y	Y	N	X
b. Non-public (Y—Yes; N—No; I—Incomplete)	I	I	I	I			N		I	I	I	I	I	I	I
14. Coöperation—															
Bureau of Vital Statistics	Y	Y	Y	Y					Y	I	Y	I	I	I	I
Express companies	N	N	N	N					N	Y	I	I	I	I	I
Police	Y	I	I				Y		Y	Y	I	I	I	I	I
Social agencies	I	I	I	I			Y		I	I	Y	I	I	I	I

Types of Enumeration: (1) Check lists of school population. (2) House-to-house canvass. (3) House-to-house canvass with school enrollment as check.

tending school. Last year 500 non-attendants were discovered. No effort had been made to determine their non-attendance.

Where an enumeration was required by law all the cities, with the exception of City B, set the last months of the school year as the time for taking the census. This gave the attendance department time to tabulate the results before the opening of the next school term. City B took its enumeration from October to March. No city, however, made any attempt to use at the opening of a new school term the data obtained.

City C claimed a continuing census in compliance with the state law. After comparing the parochial school census file, card by card, with the parochial school enrollment it was found that out of the parochial school enrollment of 754 children 224 or 30 per cent were in school without their names appearing on the census files. Of the 604 parochial school cards in the census file 113, or 19 per cent, were not found in the school enrollment. In view of these discrepancies one could not be justified in calling it a continuing census.

Although City D was officially accredited with a continuing census the writer was informed that there was no necessity of making a careful examination to determine the accuracy of the census, as it was impossible to keep up the census files without clerical assistance.

A random sampling of 81 dismissal reports of City D when compared with the census files showed the following:

No cards for address given......................	10
Different names in census for address given.......	2
No cards for pupils	28
Cards of dismissed pupils still in file.............	15
Census and cards agreed	26

Out of a random sampling of 120 names on school enrollment compared with the census files, the cards for 72 pupils were found recorded and 48 were not found in the census. Further investigation was deemed unnecessary in view of the large packages of census changes that for months had remained unrecorded.

Group III.—The growth of the modern city census out of the state census for determining state appropriation is shown from the present status of the school census of Cities D to H, in a state which formerly took a census but does so no longer. The law reads: "The Board of Education of any school district may cause to be taken an exact census of all children." The five cities mentioned above had not taken a census since 1919. City D was endeavoring to maintain a continuing census under hopeless handicaps and acknowledges its failure. The need for a census in the other cities had apparently ceased, since the state appropriation is now based upon attendance and not upon the total number, or potential school population. The school authorities in other cities of the state evidently failed to recognize the fact that a regular census always increased the number of children enrolled and consequently increased their quota of state appropriation on the basis of school attendance.

There was the greatest confidence on the part of school superintendents in these cities that every child in the city was in school. One superintendent expressed his conclusions with the statement that "about 20 per cent of the city's population should be in school and that is about what ours is." The attendance officers, however, did not express the same confidence. One city of the group had seriously discussed the advisability of establishing a continuing census.

REVISION AND CHECKING OF CENSUS

Cities B, K, and M completed their census for determining state apportionment and then laid the census away until the time came for the next census. City N made a futile attempt to check the school enrollment with the census but did not get it completely checked before it was time for the next census to be started. City M claimed the census was checked, but this was later admitted to be incorrect after the examination of the original census blanks showed no evidence of checking. The checking claimed was merely the reading of the names of the census and the recording of the number under the age-group distributions required by the state report.

Not one city had any method of checking the enumeration with a house file or other enumeration of the city. City K alone recorded the vacant houses and those unoccupied during the time of enumeration, but made no further investigation of these records except in cases where the school enrollment showed pupils in school who were not enumerated. In such cases many of the occupants of these houses were located.

City K was the only city which had checked its census with the Federal Census and had found that its house-to-house school enumeration had corresponded closely with it. This enumeration, however, had been greatly increased by the number not found in the house-to-house canvass but included in the school enrollment census. City K was the one city which had made a house-to-house canvass and a separate school enrollment census. The large number of errors discovered in the house-to-house method showed the necessity of checking carefully with the total school enrollment.

Six cities made some sort of revision of the census. Five of those having an annual census waited for the next census to make whatever revision was made. The others, as shown in Table IX, had reports at varying intervals, some of which were used and some discarded entirely. City I had regular monthly reports of change of address but made no attempt to correct the census cards. Out of all the cities studied City A had the only organized continuing revision of its census. The results of its efforts were shown in its ability at the end of the year to check one half of the schools exactly with the census. Before fully organizing this revision not one of the school enrollments had checked with the census and one school had had over two hundred discrepancies.

The outstanding weaknesses in the present administration of school census as shown by inquiries, reports, and the detailed investigations of fifteen cities are:

1. Incomplete and inaccurate information regarding total school population.
2. The information obtained is temporary and not continuing and up-to-date.
3. The actual school population is not adequately or regularly checked with the school enrollment.
4. There is lack of full coöperation between the school authorities and the non-public schools, making the so-called continuing census in most cities merely a continuing registration of public school enrollment.
5. The school rather than the home is made the basis of information for the so-called census.

6. There is lack of any definite program of organized up-keep for a continuing census.
7. The state school census laws are not in some states mandatory, so no census is now taken in these cities.
8. The school census is used as a basis for a state appropriation for school funds rather than for the full enforcement of the compulsory school laws and child labor laws.
9. Many school authorities see no necessity for more accurate continuing information regarding the school population for which they are legally responsible.
10. In general there is failure on the part of school and community agencies to coöperate with the administrative officers in maintaining accurate school population statistics.
11. Laxity on the part of school administrators causes failure to secure the full coöperation of all schools, public and non-public, or to seek remedial measures to bring about a conformity to the compulsory school attendance and child labor laws.

METHOD OF CONTINUING CENSUS RECOMMENDED

A complete child accounting for the purpose of securing the full quota of state revenue to which the city may be entitled—and certainly for enforcing the compulsory education laws as well as for providing the optimum educational service—requires an uninterrupted and constant individual record for every child. It matters not what may be the age-span required by the state census or by the community ideals as to the ages for which it should be responsible, the principle of the continuing census is to make available at all times the facts for the ages locally necessary or desirable.

State census requirements are so different in age-spans, kind of information required, and blanks to be used that a plan for a continuing census, to be of value at the present time, must be capable of adjustment to the actual and not to the ideal conditions. No state law prohibits a city from having as complete a child accounting as it desires. The more complete and accurate the original enumeration, the less difficult will it be to maintain the continuing census satisfactorily. Where the state laws require an annual census such a census will form a desirable annual check upon the work of the census department and will insure greater efficiency in maintaining it.

When cities are able to show that they are maintaining a continuing census as complete and accurate—or even more complete and accurate—than the present type of discrete enumeration, it should not be difficult to secure legislation in favor of the continuing form of census.

The task involved in maintaining a continuing census will vary with the stability of the population. In growing cities or in cities with rapidly shifting populations the work of the census department will be greater than in a city where there is a large home-ownership population. In the former cities it may be necessary to employ the greater part or all of the time of one attendance officer in making special investigations, while in the latter city the regular attendance officer on the basis of one officer to each three thousand enrollment will be able to do the work.

Every phase of the "continuing census" recommended has as its object the accomplishment of the following purposes:

1. A constant and accurate file of every house occupied or unoccupied within the jurisdiction of the school board, with the names and ages of all occupants of school census ages.
2. Easily accessible information regarding name, age, address, name of parent, school attended or the reason for non-attendance of every child of compulsory school age.
3. To render available for the school authorities all the information necessary for the development of a modern school system on the basis of actual needs.
4. To make it possible for the school authorities to have constantly available information regarding school population required by state laws, and such other information educationally desirable for and coöperation with other social agencies.

Experience shows that in the installation of any administrative organization adaptation to local needs must be considered. The laws requiring the coöperation of other agencies, such as moving companies, too often break down in actual practice. The coöperation of all the agencies involved must be built up by personal contacts. No procedure is recommended that has not been tried out in some form in actual practice. If any part of the method recommended seems to be unjustified because of the expenditure of time required, it may be eliminated, provided the efficiency demanded in the four purposes outlined may be met without it. The experience of others, however, shows that all are important in a properly functioning organization.

FORMS AND RECORDS RECOMMENDED

For carrying out the continuous census desired the following forms are recommended:

1. Map of the city.
2. House card.
3. Printed or typed directions for enumerators.
4. Enumeration sheet.
5. Permanent record card.
6. Follow-up card.
7. Enrollment card.
8. Lists of previously enrolled—not entered.
9. Change of address and school census correction card.
10. Daily left report.
11. Weekly summary enrollment, transfers, change of address, lefts.
12. Attendance officer's report of change of address.
13. Notice to enumerators.
14. Home information blank.
15. Special census inquiry: (*a*) Form 1; (*b*) Form 2.
16. Memorandum blank.
17. Notice label.
18. Street report.
19. Report of enumerator.
20. Physician's certificate.
21. Certificate of home instruction.
22. School census report.

DESCRIPTION AND USE OF FORMS RECOMMENDED

Form 1. City Map.—The basis and first requisite of an accurate and complete enumeration should be a map of the city giving the location, block number and street number, or boundaries, of every residence within the jurisdiction of the school authorities. Such a map must be a constant source of reference for the "house card file" which is made from it as well as for accurately following and checking the progress of the enumeration to see that every house is canvassed. With such a map and card file of every residence in the city every actual or potential home can be accounted for and the vacant houses at all times can be indicated by small signals, or separate file, to attract attention to the necessity of watchfulness for new occupants.

No doubt the time is approaching when every city of 25,000 and over will have its aërial maps. By a recent invention, "it is now possible to make an aërial map as accurate, and often more so, than the regular survey maps." In spite of the cost attached to this work, it is nevertheless a fact that photographic maps are cheaper than maps produced by other methods. The information made available is not subject to the omissions and errors that are so common in ordinary maps. They are now being used in city planning and in studying traffic conditions and they ought to prove an invaluable aid to the attendance department in forming the basic map for a development of its "house card file" and for checking the accuracy of census enumeration.[9]

The standard minimum geographic unit for the census should be the block. This unit is advisable because it may easily be built up into any size district, zoning, school or health, as community or special needs may demand.[10]

For the purpose of locating the school population definitely and correctly the city must be divided into numbered census districts or zones and each block in these districts also numbered. The number of the zones will be determined by the number of attendance officers to be employed and the boundaries should be the same as the school districts of which they are composed. For a state or general enumeration these zones may be temporarily subdivided and the work assigned by small areas, in accordance with the staff employed. This map must be checked with the "house card file."

Form 2. House Card.—The House Card is made for each house

[9] Mathes, G. H., "Fairchild Aërial Surveys." Address before Dept. Aëronautical Engineers of New York University, *New York World*, Nov. 7, 1924. Kreh and Grassman Aërial Maps of Elizabeth, N. J.
[10] Moehlman, A. B., *Child Accounting*, p. 81.

occupied or unoccupied, with block number, district or zone number and street number or boundaries when the house has no street number.

Since the information regarding vacant and occupied houses comes to the central office as "No.... X Street," less time will be required for the file clerks if the house cards are filed numerically by streets. When filed in this way a regrouping of cards will be necessary for data involving the number of houses in blocks, districts or political divisions.

In some cases it has been found valuable to the board of education, in determining the location for a new building, to have a cross file of the school population by blocks. By means of such a file the exact number of persons of the ages desired or of those actually in school may be quickly determined in any block or group of blocks. Unless such information is in continuous demand the filing of the house cards by streets can be made to readily serve this purpose. When needed the information is obtainable without the necessity of maintaining another file.

FORM 2. HOUSE CARD

HOUSE CARD	City of...........................	
Date.................................		
Zone ...... Block .... Street .... No.......		
Apartment .... Floor		
Father .... Age..... Nationality		
(Last name, First name)		
Mother .... Age..... Nationality		
Children	Age	Date of Birth
....		
....		
....		
....		
....		

[*Reverse side used for another family in same house.*]

This card will first be made from the enumeration sheets as they are completed and returned by the enumerators. The house is checked on the map and the progress of the enumeration accurately determined. Any house not reported will be noted and the enumerator held responsible for the complete information. Any house not appearing on the map and reported by the enumerator will be added. The card should allow for the addition of new names and for more than one family in a house. In large cities more than one card might be required. A new card should be filled out for every new house constructed as reported by attendance officers or obtained from the continued checking of building permits issued and other sources. Cards for unoccupied houses are filed with attached signals or in a separate file by streets. The attendance officer should be held responsible for the immediate reporting of changing occupancy.

Form 3. Directions for Enumerators.—Accuracy cannot be expected from enumerators unless they are fully informed regarding the data to be obtained, the manner of questioning whereby the number of errors may be reduced, and the meaning and use of the code employed. Detailed explanations must be given by oral and printed instructions. These directions must cover every detail of the enumerator's duties as determined by the ages to be enumerated, the information called for, and the time and manner of returning enumeration sheets.

Form 4. Enumeration Sheet.—An Enumeration Sheet is used for gathering the information, both that required by law and that deemed essential for complete educational service. The form shown in Figure III, or one closely resembling it, has been found in use in many cities. Another column for the name or number of the school the child attends may be added or this may be expressed as a fraction on the blank. If the fraction is used the numerator indicates the kind of school and the denominator the particular school. Such information will later be found helpful in making use of the Follow-up Cards.

After the enumeration sheets have been completed they are filed in a loose-leaf binder by blocks and zones to become the source book for the House Cards, Permanent Census Cards, Follow-up Cards, and Special Inquiry Cards. The Enumeration Sheets are checked after these records are made. The names discovered from school enrollment and not enumerated should be added to the proper sheet and checked when the other records have been completed and filed.

The Enumeration Sheet should provide the following entries for every child from 1 day to 20 years inclusive:

1. Full name of child.
2. Date of birth with year, month and day.
3. Evidence of birth, as birth certificate, baptismal certificate or passport.
4. Sex.
5. Birthplace (country), also birthplace of parents or guardian.
6. Citizenship.
7. Residence, street and number.
8. School and kind of school child is attending.
9. Facts of employment if employed and not in school.
10. Physical condition, deaf, dumb, blind, cripple, etc.
11. Facts regarding non-enrollment and not employed.
12. Houses from which no children are reported,—block number.
13. House closed,—for the day, the summer, vacant.

If further information is desired the form may include:

Information about house—
  a. Parental status.
  b. Home owned or rented.
  c. Language in home.

Whatever form is used, a cord, as shown in Figure III, is necessary to facilitate the work.

Form 5. Permanent Census Card.—This card must be a copy of all the information entered upon the Enumeration Sheet. As soon as the Enumeration Sheet is complete these cards are made out at the central office and filed alphabetically. The card becomes the permanent continuing registration or census record of the individual. The card, as shown in Figure IV, provides for future changes of address and for the employment record after leaving school. This record is kept up to date by entering all changes reported to the attendance department. New cards must be made for all those becoming of census age and cards must be withdrawn after the individual attains the age limit. It is with this file that the school enrollment of all schools, public, private and parochial, must be checked. Upon the thoroughness and promptness of this checking and upon the completeness and accuracy of its up-keep depends the value of the census as a factor in safeguarding the enrollment in school of every child of compulsory school age.

The form shown in Figure IV is based upon the enumeration sheet shown in Figure III.

Changes in this file can be more readily and quickly made if a visible filing system is used for the Permanent Census Card. There are many advantages in such a system. Cards are easily

Fig. III

FORM 4. ENUMERATION SHEET

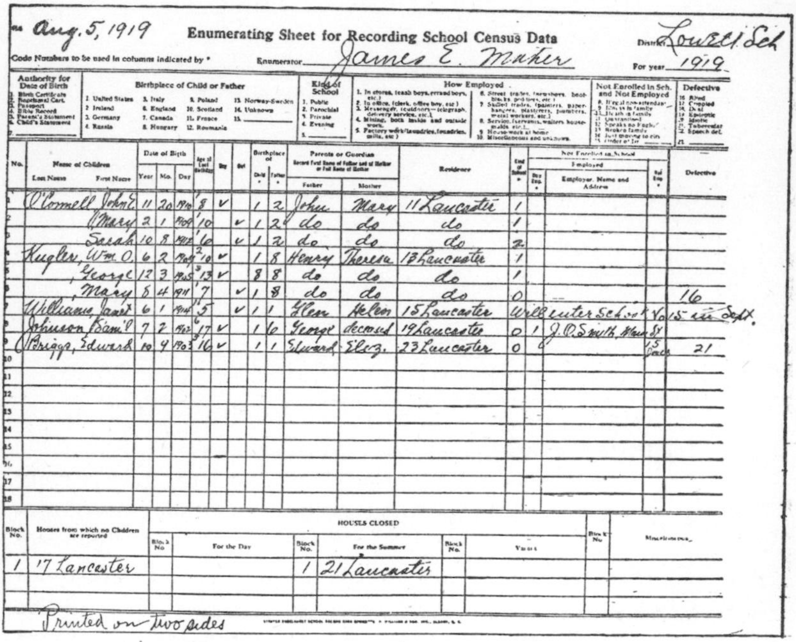
Date Aug. 5, 1919 — Enumerating Sheet for Recording School Census Data — District Lowell Sch

Code Numbers to be used in columns indicated by * — Enumerator James E. Maher — For year 1919

Authority for Date of Birth: 1. Birth Certificate 2. Baptismal Cert. 3. Passport 4. Bible Record 5. Parent's Statement 6. Child's Statement 7. ____

Birthplace of Child or Father: 1. United States 2. Ireland 3. Germany 4. Russia 5. Italy 6. England 7. Canada 8. Hungary 9. Poland 10. Scotland 11. France 12. Roumania 13. Norway-Sweden 14. Unknown 15. ____

Kind of School: 1. Public 2. Parochial 3. Private 4. Evening 5. ____

How Employed: 1. In stores, (cash boys, errand boys, etc.) 2. In office, (clerk, office boy, etc.) 3. Messenger, (outdoors—telegraph, delivery service, etc.) 4. Mining, both inside and outside work. 5. Factory work (laundries, foundries, mills, etc.) 6. Street trades, (newsboys, bootblacks, peddlers, etc.) 7. Skilled trades, (painters, paperhangers, plasterers, plumbers, metal workers, etc.) 8. Service, (servants, waiters, housemaids, etc.) 9. House-work at home 10. Miscellaneous and unknown.

Not Enrolled in Sch. and Not Employed: 8. Illegal non-attendant 9. Illness in family 11. Health in family [illegible] Quarantined 12. Speaks no English 13. Broken family 14. Just moving to city 15. Under or [illegible]

Defective: 16. Blind 17. Crippled 18. Deaf 19. Epileptic [illegible] Idiotic [illegible] Tubercular [illegible] Speech def. 21. ____

No.	Last Name	First Name	Year	Mo.	Day	Age at Last Birthday	Boy	Girl	Birthplace of Child *	Birthplace of Father *	Father	Mother	Residence	Kind of School *	Day Emp. *	Employer, Name and Address	Ref. Emp. *	Defective
1	O'Connell	John E.	11	20	1910	8	✓		1	2	John	Mary	11 Lancaster	1				
2		Mary	2	1	1909	10		✓	1	2	do	do	do	1				
3		Sarah	10	8	1912	6		✓	1	2	do	do	do	2				
4	Kugler,	Wm. O.	6	2	1909	2 10	✓		1	8	Henry	Theresa	13 Lancaster	1				
5		George	12	3	1905	3 13	✓		8	8	do	do	do	1				
6		Mary	8	4	1911	7		✓	1	8	do	do	do	0				16
7	Williams,	Janet	6	1	1914	5		✓	1	1	Glen	Helen	15 Lancaster	Will enter School Nov 15				15 Sept.
8	Johnson,	Sam'l	7	2	1902	6 17	✓		1	6	George	deceased	19 Lancaster	0	1	J. O. Smith, Main St.		
9	Briggs,	Edward	10	4	1903	3 16	✓		1	1	Edward	Eliz.	23 Lancaster	0			15 [illegible]	21
10																		
11																		
12																		
13																		
14																		
15																		
16																		
17																		
18																		

HOUSES CLOSED

Block No.	Houses from which no Children are reported	Block No.	For the Day	Block No.	For the Summer	Block No.	Vacant	Block No.	Miscellaneous
1	17 Lancaster			1	21 Lancaster				

Printed on two sides

located, the danger of misplacing or losing them is eliminated, and data for state or local reports may be made without removing cards from the file.

When local conditions make it difficult to obtain enrollment cards from non-public schools, the enrollment lists, usually given with names, address and date of birth, should be checked with the Permanent Census Cards, Form 5. Follow-up Cards and inquiry sheets should be used to obtain complete information about those enrolled who are not on file.

A separate file of these cards for all children not attending school as required by the school laws should be used as the basis for constant study, investigation, and check. If these cards are filed by street numbers, they are more readily assigned to the proper attendance officers for checking. Changes must be made in this file whenever the regular permanent census cards are cor-

Fɪɢ. IV.

FORM 5.   PERMANENT CENSUS CARD

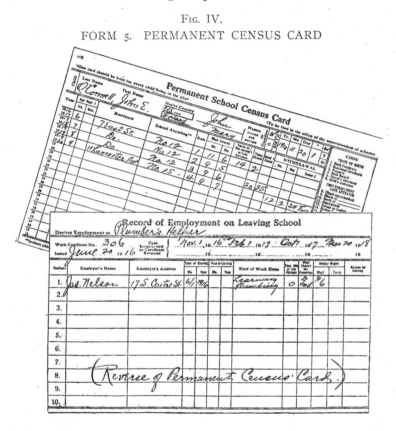

rected. This file will be made after all Follow-up Cards have been checked.

Form 6. Follow-Up Cards.—When the enumeration is taken, either the original or the later enumeration made by attendance officers, the names of those of legal school age not attending school must be investigated. After making a permanent census card a

Follow-up Card should be filled out and filed for immediate investigation. This card should give:

Name, age, date of birth, sex, race.
Old address, number, street, floor, apartment.
New address, number, street, floor, apartment (if moved).
Parent or guardian.

Cause of Investigation	*Result of Investigation*

Cause of Investigation

1. Under compulsory years
2. Illegal non-attendant
3. Temporarily excused
4. Temporarily unemployed
5. Permanently incapacitated
6. Illegally employed
   Name
   Address
7. Name on sheet but no card on file
8. Defective
(The investigator checks the item involved. Items requiring additional information are starred.)

Result of Investigation

I. 1. Found enrolled
    2. Ordered to enroll
    3. Legally excused
II. 1. Truant and returned
    2. Found enrolled
    3. Other disposition
III. 1. Doctor's certificate
     2. Returned to school
IV. 1. Referred to Probation Office
    2. Returned to school
V. 1. Referred to special school visitor
    2. Referred to psychological laboratory
    3. Referred to Juvenile Court
    4. Referred to other agency
VI. 1. Referred to Working Certificate Office
    2. Referred to school
VII. 1. Found in school indicated
     2. Not enrolled in school
     3. Moved during census
VIII. 1. Referred to school visitor
      2. Referred to Board of Health
      3. Referred to Psychological Laboratory
      4. Doctor's certificate on file

When the card is given to the attendance officer, a memorandum should be retained at the office to insure return of card. This may be done by placing a colored signal on the Permanent Census Card to be removed when the case is completed. The Permanent Census Card is corrected in accordance with the information returned. The follow-up for "houses closed" at the time of enumeration should be made on the Home Information Blank, Form 14, or by personal investigation.

Form 7. Enrollment Card.—A duplicate of the Enrollment Card from every public, parochial and private school, as shown in Form 7, should be sent to the census department as soon as possible after the opening of school in September in order to check immediately the school enrollment with the census cards.

This card should contain:

1. Name and number of the school.
2. Name of pupil and race, W. B. Y.
3. Date of entrance.
4. Date of vaccination.
5. Telephone number.
6. Birthplace of pupil and date of birth in years, months, days.
7. The last school attended is important in order to trace previous enrollment of child and to check any failure for prompt enrollment from elementary to high school and continuation school or from non-public to public school.
8. The assignment by grade, class and room.
9. The withdrawal date.
10. The cause of withdrawal.
11. The name of parent or guardian and where employed.
12. The birthplace of father and mother.
13. The name of the teacher.

The reverse side of this card should contain the name, age, school attended, if not in school why, for the brothers and sisters and any others living in the family between the ages of one day and twenty years inclusive.

These cards are filled out by the child under the direction of the classroom teacher, placed in alphabetical order, and sent to the principal's office. The cards for the entire school are then collected alphabetically and sent to the attendance department where they are filed alphabetically by schools. This becomes the cumulative enrollment for the year of all schools, public and non-public.

From this file additions to the Permanent Census Card and House Card must be made and the names given of those not previously on file in the family investigated, and new cards made out. All pupils not previously enrolled in another city school during the year must fill out this card upon enrollment. These should then be forwarded to the attendance department. All other admissions will be cared for by the Admission, Transfer and Dismissal form.

FORM 7. ENROLLMENT CARD

```
ENROLLMENT CARD              City of............................
School ..................... Date ...........................
                                                 W  ...........
Name of pupil...............................Race B  ...........
                                           (Check) Y  ...........
Date of entrance....................Vaccinated (yr)................
Residence ........................... Telephone ...................
Birthplace .......................... Date of birth ...............
Last school attended ........................................
Assignment: Grade ............. class ............ room ...........
Withdrawal date ................... Teacher ......................
Cause ......................................................
Parent or guardian................. Employed where................
Father's birthplace................... Mother's....................
```

[Reverse of the above card.]

Give below names and ages of brothers and sisters and any others living
in family between ages of ...... and ......

Name	Age	School Attended	If not in school WHY?

[White card for girls. Yellow card for boys.]

All persons listed on the back of enrollment cards must be investigated by checking with the Permanent Census Card or by a personal visit of the enumerator.

Form 8. Lists of Previously Enrolled, Not Entered.—Every city studied reported that one of its chief sources of loss was the failure of the elementary school and the high school to check up immediately the list of elementary school graduates in order to determine the names of those who had failed to report and who were either employed without working papers or were not employed and non-attendant.

. There should be no excuse for this failure to fully coöperate with the attendance service. The duplicate enrollment cards from all schools will be the complete check upon all non-attendants, but much time will be saved and assistance rendered if all schools check their September enrollment with their June enrollment, and the lists of those who have been promoted to one school from another school, or who by graduation are entitled and expected to be enrolled. The attendance officer will then be in a position to investigate immediately all discrepancies. All the information required will be the name, school, age, grade and residence of pupil. The promptness with which these lists are prepared, investigated and acted upon will greatly affect future cases of late entrance.

Form 9. Change of Address and School Census Correction Card.—One source of loss in attendance and one cause of the breaking down of the continuing census is the failure to receive prompt and regular reports of changes of address, new enrollments and "left" reports. To obviate these losses daily reports should be required of all schools, public, parochial and private, on the forms given below. They should be mailed to the attendance department or given to the attendance officer daily. They are checked with the census and filed by schools to be checked against the weekly and monthly reports of the schools as to totals. These will also serve as checks one against the other and against transfers. This card should be used when any change is made in the school record of the name or date of birth of any pupil. The form and content are shown below.

FORM 9. CHANGE OF ADDRESS AND CENSUS
CORRECTION CARD

CHANGE OF ADDRESS AND CENSUS CORRECTION

City...........................

To be sent to the Attendance Department when a child changes his address but not his school.

Child's given name......Surname......Grade....Date of birth........

Former address.................... Present address..................

Correction, Name.................... Date of birth...................

Father's name......... or Guardian........ Mother's name.........

Date............................. School.......................

Form 10. Daily "Left" Reports.—This report must be filled out and sent to the attendance department as soon as a child leaves school. It may be used in the following form.

FORM 10. DAILY "LEFT" REPORT

DAILY LEFT REPORT   City...............................

    To be sent to Attendance Department on the day pupil leaves.

Name................... Class............Date of birth.............
Old address.....................New address......................
Reason for leaving: ....
A. D. P. Card mailed   (Check method used)   Sent by child
Name of Father................... Name of Mother.................
                                      School.................

Form 11. Weekly Summary: Enrollment, Transfers, Changes of Address, Lefts.—Each week the schools should send to the attendance office an Enrollment Report giving a summary of all pupils received by transfers, new enrollments, pupils to whom transfers were given, pupils who have left school and pupils who have changed their addresses. These reports should be checked with the daily reports on Forms 7, 9, and 10. The report can be made cumulative for the year by giving the number previously reported and totals. This will obviate the necessity of an annual report by schools and will enable the attendance department to make a report at any time for the school system. The reports should be filed by schools and a cumulative record, distributed by schools, maintained for the city. The form is shown on page 53.

Form 12. Attendance Officer's Report of Change of Address. —In canvassing a street or in the daily routine of attendance service it will be necessary for the attendance officer to report all changes of address. All such changes are returned to the office on Form 12. This card contains the names of the children in a family, also the present and former addresses and the present school attended. The Permanent Record, the House Card and the Enrollment Card are corrected by census clerks so as to show changes, especially the changes of address. The Change of

FORM 11. WEEKLY SUMMARY

ENROLLMENT REPORT City.............................

School.................... Week ending..................... 192...

Pupils Received by Transfer

Name of pupil Residence School from which transferred Grade Date

....

Previously reported......... Total.........

New Enrollments

Name of pupil   Residence   Date of enrollment

.....................·.......... ....

Previously reported......... Total.........

Pupils to Whom Transfers Were Given

Name of pupil Residence Date School to which transferred Grade

....

Previously reported......... Total.........

Pupils Who Have Left School

Name of pupil   Residence   Date of leaving   Reason for leaving

....

Previously reported......... Total.........

Pupils Who Change Their Addresses

Name of pupil Change from street & number Change to street, number

....·.......

Previously reported......... Total.........

Principal..............................

Address Card should be filed alphabetically. Such cards, however, would be of little value after a year's time.

In many instances such changes will already have been made through information received from the daily change of address reports returned by the school. The promptness of the school and that of the attendance officer in discovering such changes and in making reports will thus be brought into contrast.

This form contains the changes discovered by the attendance officer in canvassing his district. It should be in two colors; one color for

1. Changes of address
2. Those moved out of the city

and the other color for

1. Those who have moved into the city
2. Those becoming of census age
3. Other new records

Form 12 contains the following information:

1. The date when filled out
2. The new address, street and number
3. Parent's name
4. The first name and age of all children of census age
5. The former address, street and number
6. The school attended
7. The district number
8. The signature or initials of officer

Form 13. Notice to Enumerators.—This blank is used in cases where an immediate investigation cannot be made after information has been received from schools or attendance officers or from other sources, giving a new address for a child. The blank is attached to the house card of the new address until the street is canvassed. When the change of address card is received the record is removed from the former house card file and recorded at the present address. This blank is then destroyed. A suitable form follows.

FORM 13. NOTICE TO ENUMERATORS

City.............................

NOTICE

Look up children of this family. They should be at this address. If they have moved to another street and number make the change of address on this card, otherwise check below.

Can't locate ☐   Family name ....

Street..................... No.......

Moved away ☐   New address ....

Form 14. Home Information Blank.—This blank is mailed to or left at the home of a family whom the census officer has been unable to find at home. The following information should be called for:

FORM 14. HOME INFORMATION BLANK

"To the Parent or Guardian:

The information called for in this blank is required by law. You are requested to answer the following questions with reference to parent or guardian and for each child under twenty-one years of age and mail this report in the enclosed envelope immediately.

I hereby certify that the statements given below are correct.

Signed....................................

1. Residence No......Street...............Date....................
2. Last name of father or guardian.............First name..........
3. Birthplace of father.........................Years in U.S.....
4. Children under twenty years..................................
5. Last name of each child.................................••.......
6. First name of each child.......................................
7. Birthplace (country) of each child.............................
8. Child's date of birth, month..............day.......year.........
9. What school does child attend..................................
10. If child does not attend regularly give reason..................

The following questions are to be answered only when children are or have been employed.

1. Is the boy (or girl) employed............
2. How many years has he (or she) been employed..............
3. Has he (or she) a working certificate..........
4. Give name of present employer..................................
5. Give address of present employer...............................
6. How long has the boy (or girl) been employed there............

NOTE.—This blank should be ruled for four spaces to allow for information for at least four children in a family.

The information thus secured will be transferred to the Permanent Census Card and the House Card by the clerks at the central office and the Attendance Card and non-attendance file checked. The use of this card will avoid loss of time of the attendance officer.

Form 15. Special Census Inquiry No. 1.—When the department wishes information regarding children of any family reported to them for any reason, by the schools or other sources, a Special Census Inquiry should be issued to the enumerator requesting him to prepare a Permanent Census Card for all the children in that family whose name and address appear on the blank. Whatever facts are known in the office are written on the blanks for the guidance of the enumerator. Upon receipt of the information both the original and the carbon copies, which had been retained as a memorandum that such inquiry had been issued, are destroyed. The form given below shows the type of information usually given to the attendance officer.

FORM 15. SPECIAL CENSUS INQUIRY NO. 1

SPECIAL CENSUS INQUIRY No. 1.   City.......................

Family name....................Street....................No.......

First Name	Date of Birth	School Attended	Work Certificate
....	....	....	....
....	....	....	....
....	....	....	....
....	....	....	....
....	....	....	....

Reported by...............................

Special Inquiry No. 2.—Whenever a child of school age, but not attending school, is reported to the central office, by a school or by any source whatever, Form No. 2 should be made in duplicate, the original being kept at the attendance office and the duplicate given to an attendance officer who investigates and sees that the child attends school. Admission of the child should be checked with the Daily Enrollment Slip from the school to which the child was taken.

This form contains the following information:

FORM 15 (*Continued*). SPECIAL CENSUS INQUIRY NO. 2

SPECIAL CENSUS INQUIRY No. 2.

City of.......................   Date.........................

Name.........................   Born, Mo.......Day.....Yr......

Address................. Left............School at the......Grade

Parent's name.................... Attending... N.W.C....Absence.....

Employed by...................... No. of W. C...................

Employer's address..........Kind of work............to............

Remarks ....

Disposition ....

Signed...................................

If mentally or physically unable to attend school or if taught at home, a doctor's certificate or a certificate of "home instruction" is required. All the information asked for is easily noted and the blank is returned to the office. The facts given are transferred to a Permanent Census Card and other records and the blank filed alphabetically. This form may also be used in the same way for violations of the Child Labor Law, local or otherwise. It enables the department to determine the school whose laxity of reports has made non-attendance possible.

Form 16. Memorandum Blank.—A loose-leaf memorandum book should be provided for the use of the attendance officer to record the names of families which were not located in canvassing the street. After the card in the "house file" has been changed by the clerk in the central office a House Card with the name of the family is placed in a "search file" for inquiry as to new address. When this new address has been found the memorandum is destroyed.

Form 17. Notice Label.—If the Permanent Record Card contains any questionable data as to age, residence, or spelling of name, a small label 2″ x 2″, printed in red, may be attached to the Permanent Census Card and the enumerator asked to get a new Permanent Census Card. These cards should be in evidence until a new card is obtained. The label should read: *"Notice.*—Secure a new record for this child."

Form 18. Street Report.—This is prepared in the census department for each street in the census district and is given to the enumerator with the House Cards of the streets in his district to be canvassed. After he has canvassed a street he enters the changes discovered and turns the new records in with the old records and reports of changes. This report is shown on page 58.

With the report of the canvass the canvasser must hand in Change of Address Cards (Form 9) for all the items. The first two will be for changes of cards already in the file and the last three for new cards; therefore, a different colored card should be used for the two sets of items. With his report the officer returns the House Cards for the street to which he had been assigned. After the reports have been checked, Form 18 is filed chronologically in the proper census district so as to determine

FORM 18. CENSUS STREET REPORT

| CENSUS STREET REPORT | | | City of...................... | | | | |
| Street.................From No........to No........Zone......... | | | | | | | |
Date of canvass	Change of address	Moved from city	Moved into city	Became ...yrs. old	Other new records	Total reports	Officers' name
....	....	....	....	......	......	......	....
....	....	....	....	......	......	......	....
....	....	....	....	......	......	......	....
....	....	....	....	......	......	......	....
....	....	....	....	......	......	......	....
....	....	....	....	......	......	......	....
....	....	....	....	......	......	......	....
....	....	....	....	......	......	......	....
Total							

the month of the next canvass of that street. The frequency of canvass may be at any interval locally considered necessary. It will be dependent upon the type of homes on the street and the size of the staff employed. With the schools properly co-operating one complete canvass each six months should be adequate.

Form 19. Report of Enumerator.—The daily report of the census work performed by the attendance officer should be indicated on this form. All the census information obtained by the attendance officer while investigating absentees or doing field work should be indicated on this blank and the cards and records made. The total cases enumerated or checked become a part of the attendance officer's daily report of attendance work.

FORM 19. DAILY ENUMERATION REPORT

| DAILY ENUMERATION REPORT | | | City of...................... | | | |
| Zone...........Officer's Name...................Date........... | | | | | | |
Street	Change of address	Moved from city	Moved into city	Became ...yrs. old	Other new records	Total reports
....	....	....	....	......	....	......
....	....	....	....	......	....	......
Total						

Form 20. Physician's Certificate.—When children are permanently or temporarily excused from school attendance because of physical or mental disability, a physician's certificate should be

required. This certificate provides for the information shown in the following form.

FORM 20. PHYSICIAN'S CERTIFICATE

```
City of.................... Date........................
            PHYSICIAN'S CERTIFICATE        No......

This is to certify that...........................age.....
residence...................pupil at...............school
should be excused from attendance for.....months or per-
manently because of the following disabilities............
....................................................................
....................................................................
.......................M.D. .................Address

Date of investigation.........Approved.....Rejected.....
...........................M. D., School Physician
```

If it is desirable that further investigation be made, a space is given for the date of investigation with approval or rejection by the school physician. The cards for permanent and temporary certificates should be filed alphabetically in separate files. The numbers are recorded on the Permanent Census Cards and in the file of non-attendants. In the file of the temporary certificates a signal should be attached for the month when return is expected. This forms a "suspension file or register" that must be checked weekly to insure return of those temporarily excused.

A daily record of date, number, name, address, and whether temporary or permanent, permits of a summary of certificates granted during any period of time.

Form 21. Certificate of Home Instruction.—A form similar to Form 20 should be required from all parents with children of compulsory school age who are receiving home instruction. This certificate should include:

1. The date of certificate
2. Name, age and residence of child
3. Name of person by whom instruction is given
4. The signature of the child's parent
5. Approval by the superintendent or other in authority
6. Signature of instructor
7. List of school subjects taught
8. Probable duration of home instruction

These cards are filed alphabetically after a record is made on the Permanent Census Cards and the non-attendant cards.

Our sources of census records as given above are, (*a*) enumeration sheets, (*b*) duplicate copies of entrance records of all public, private and parochial schools, (*c*) home information inquiry, (*d*) the reverse portion of all enrollment cards from public and private schools, and (*e*) constant investigation by attendance officers.

To these sources we should add the moving lists obtained by personal visitation to transfer companies, the lists of inmates and information from institutions for the housing of children, such as orphanages, and the lists of births and deaths from the Bureau of Vital Statistics.

Form 22. School Census Report.—In three of the cities studied (Cities A, I, and J) regular census reports from classroom teachers are called for. Denver, Colo., and Newark, N. J., make use of a juvenile organization consisting of a child representative in each block. This representative reports to the attendance officer through the teacher all moves into or out of the block. Such information is often helpful in enabling the attendance officer to make an early discovery of changes of address which have been overlooked. For this service the form shown below will serve.

FORM 22. SCHOOL CENSUS REPORT

```
┌─────────────────────────────────────────────────────────┐
│ SCHOOL CENSUS REPORT      City of.....................   │
│ School...................  Date.......................   │
│ ....................moved into...................St.     │
│ ....................moved out of.................St.     │
│ Remarks ..............................................   │
│ School Representative.................................   │
└─────────────────────────────────────────────────────────┘
```

The tabulation of the information available must be capable of clear interpretation. Mere tabulations are a waste of time and money. They must be of some educational service. If forms and records contain identical or similar types of information, this information should be in the same order on both the forms and the records to aid transferring of items and to facilitate tabulation. The large cities have found from experience that the cost of tabulation by clerical staff can be reduced and the tabulation made more quickly and accurately by the use of tabulating machines. There seems to be no valid reason why all the items in a census file should be tabulated every year. At times one type of information may be desired and later other information may be important. From the records given this can be obtained when needed. The object of the census is not to display interesting statistics but to further the educational interests of the children of the community.

Other forms than those described above may be used, but the purposes of the census will be attained by those given provided they are used as designed, the investigations and reports promptly checked, and the changes in the respective files made.

After the original enumeration is completed the attendance officers have Saturday mornings and school holidays for canvassing their districts. Such a program presupposed a twelve months' program with a two weeks' vacation for the officers. One officer can enumerate from 5,000 to 7,000 names in approximately six weeks and its equivalent by one day a week during the year.[11]

On a basis of one regular officer to 3,000 pupils, it is believed that a continuing census can be maintained and an annual summer canvass of all the districts made and checked before the opening of the school year. The continuing census during the year should so facilitate the summer canvass that the time required for its completion would be greatly reduced and a greater accuracy assured.

When such a program is adopted the law need no longer be ignored as too difficult of execution, and the census will not be merely compiled and forgotten.

The installation of a continuing census requires a higher type of executive efficiency than does the kind of census generally taken. The work is more complicated and the expense will be greater, but after the system is once organized the work becomes a routine keeping of data up to date, checked by constant, partial or complete reënumerations. Its value as a means of better educational administration can be far greater than its increased cost.

[11] Haney, J. D., *Registration of City School Children*, p. 118.

City reports show that the increased cost of a more adequate census brings in financial returns in excess of the expenditure made.[12]

[12] Denver, Colorado. Monograph No. 8, 1924, p. 2: "Additional names yielded $35,000 to the school district. This amount is more than the expense of the entire census and attendance department for the year 1922–23."

CHAPTER IV

REGULARITY OF ATTENDANCE

The next problem in attendance, after knowing the location and the number of children of compulsory school age and getting them in school, is to insure the regularity of their attendance. As a people we have had little reason to be proud of our record as shown by bulletin after bulletin issued by the federal government giving the country-wide conditions.

Our task in investigating the regularity of attendance in the cities studied was to determine the following:

1. The provision made for reporting absence to attendance department.
2. The type of absences reported and the information offered to attendance officer regarding absentees in order that he might render intelligent service.
3. The cumulative records maintained of previous absences as necessary to the proper treatment of case.
4. A study of the system of transfers with the loss of (a) attendance, (b) grade, and (c) school records. Also the responsibility for insuring prompt transfers from one school to another.
5. A study of dismissals or pupils dropped from roll.
6. The method employed in measuring regularity of attendance.
7. The policies that should prevail in securing regularity of attendance.
8. A description of the forms, records, and reports recommended for enforcing these policies.

There is now almost unanimous practice throughout the United States requiring continuity of school attendance regardless of the legal number of compulsory school days. By 1918 there were only six states in which this practice did not prevail.[1]

[1] Bonner, H. R., U. S. Department of Education, Bulletin No. 11, 1918, p. 86.

The compulsory education law, however, is often weak in making no provision for the reporting of absentees to the attendance department. The requirements in different states vary from no regulations to a daily report of all children absent without lawful excuse. The effectiveness of any compulsory attendance law largely depends upon the promptness with which the teacher reports:

1. Cases of known or suspected truancy.
2. Unexcused absences.
3. Absences where there is any suspicion of poverty or need of help of any kind.

Method of Reporting Absences.—The method of reporting absences, the time allowed to elapse before absences are reported, as well as the type of cases reported, have a most important bearing upon the service the attendance department is able to render. Prompt, regular, systematic investigation of all absences not properly accounted for is the very basis of any solution of non-attendance.

City B stands out in contrast with all the others, because of its inability to make use of the telephone in attendance service. Twenty-eight, or about one fifth of all the schools, with an attendance of 18,000 pupils, were directly accessible by telephone. The 108 schools with an attendance approximating 20,000 pupils could only be reached by personal visits or by messengers sent out from the telephone in a nearby home or grocery store at the request of the attendance department. Less than one half of the total school population is in direct contact by telephone with the attendance department. Notices of all absences were sent by mail to attendance department. Not more than one third of the absentees received personal visitation by the attendance officer. The attendance department acknowledged that by the method employed two days at least were lost before an absent child could be expected back in school from any action taken by the department.

In Cities C, F, G, H, I, and M the schools used the telephone almost exclusively for the reporting of absences to the central office or to the attendance officer. Knowing the daily route of the officer, schools could locate him even after he had begun his day's investigations.

In City I the attendance officer telephoned to the schools in a definite order, based upon his experience as to the time the principal would have the information available. As soon as he had what he considered a day's quota he called other schools for any bad cases he might have time to investigate. His report on investigated cases was made by telephone direct to the school. A memorandum book containing cases reported was the only record kept.

In City C the attendance officer followed a similar course, except that calls came to the superintendent's office and a memorandum was made for the attendance officer. Names of those investigated, with addresses and date, was the only record kept.

In City N the attendance officer received reports by mail or messenger from the schools.

Cities A, D, E, K, and L depended upon the officers to call at the schools and obtain the reports from the principal except in truancy cases where immediate investigation was required.

Cities D, E, and K endeavored to reach every school each day. but Cities A and L found it impossible to carry out such a program. They visited every school as often as possible. In City A, the records for two months showed that an average of four visits per month to each school had been made. The area to be covered is so great and the number of cases to be investigated so many—one child in every four of the school population had been reported at least once during the year—that often the outlying schools are not visited more than once in three months. Because of this infrequency of visitation the teachers report by telephone or mail. The reports of absences that were piled upon the desks of the attendance officers showed the necessary delays in investigations due to inadequate staff. No attempt had been made to determine to what extent the attendance department should shoulder the actual investigation of non-attendance.

In City O the attendance officer claimed that he had so reduced absence by the plan of using pupils to notify the parents of absentees that he was often compelled to visit schools to inquire for cases to investigate.

Type of Cases Reported.—The best evidences of the lack of an adequate number of attendance officers were the rules and practices that prevailed regarding the type of cases that should be reported.

In all cities it was understood that known truants should be reported at once. Whether the officer called each day at the school as in Cities D, E, and K, or whether he was reached by telephone as in some other cities, truant cases were always given precedence. The number of other cases reported was then based upon the capacity of the department.

City A allowed seven absences in six months. In City B, out of 140 cases it was found that an average of eight days was allowed before the case was considered important enough to be referred to the attendance officer. The range was from one day to twenty-six days.

City E allowed three days before reporting cases but claimed that many teachers did not wait that long. In some instances teachers did not report unless there were three consecutive absences. It was believed that pupils took advantage of the rule and ran as close and as often to it as they could.

In City L some principals awaited the visits of the attendance officer whose program did not permit of daily calls. Finding that the attendance was better on the days the attendance officer called, the central office regularly made changes of the program so that the pupils could not adjust their absences so easily to the days of visitation.

There was no evidence that any generally accepted principle prevailed. The schools in all cases adjusted themselves to the known ability of the department to investigate cases sent in. Emergency cases were usually reported at once until it had been found futile, as in City B where one teacher remarked, "This is the last report I shall make for he is beyond anything we can do."

Cities N and O were governed by the state law that immediate report should be made of pupils of compulsory school age who have been absent three days or six sessions without lawful excuse and thereafter for every additional unexcused absence. City N was endeavoring as best it could to live up to the principle in so far as the teachers reported the cases. There was no effort made to see if the teachers reported all cases. They reported cases up to the full capacity of the department to investigate. All other cases were left to the individual schools.

Information on Absence Reports.—The loose habits of the attendance officers in reporting and of the schools in referring cases was evident in every city where absence report forms were used. A study of reports in Cities D and E shows to what extent this prevails. The fact merely emphasizes the necessity that has been recognized in so many attendance departments, that all absence reports should pass through the hands of one person in a school, either the principal or some one under the direct supervision of the principal.

Cities D, E, G, and H used the same type of duplicate absence report form. In Cities G and H these were filled out in the attendance office upon telephone reports from the schools and gave the name and address of the absent child, the date of absence and date of report. The attendance office made notes of continued absences and special information that might help in the investigations. The duplicate, with cause of absence, was later taken or sent to the school by the attendance officer.

In City H, out of 260 forms, the total reported for six months, only twelve gave the total days absence, 148 gave no date of the return, and 112 had no exact information other than the name and address of the child absent. Fifteen, however, were noted as irregular and thirteen "truant often."

The attendance officer, to function efficiently, must have the absence reports filled out as legibly, accurately and completely as the information available at the school will permit, and the school is entitled to as complete information from the attendance department showing the results of the investigations and the final dispositions.

In Cities D and E, from a study of over 800 of these absence reports which were on forms issued by the state department we can see the attitude taken by teachers and principals as well as attendance officers towards the information that should be given by coöperating agencies in order to quickly and efficiently complete the investigation and disposition of the case under consideration.

These forms called for thirteen items of information from the reporting school and nine items from the investigating officer. The manner in which the information called for was omitted is shown in Table X.

Cities D, F, G, and H believed that an identification number was unnecessary, while City E used it as a means of identification in the principals' monthly reports to the attendance department as to the final disposition of all cases reported by the schools. In only a few cases, however, was the stated disposition of the case other than the exact statement on the form returned to the school by the attendance officer. The schools did not regularly indicate the date of return and as the original forms were filed alphabetically these numbers were of little or no use. The information designating whether the child was absent, truant or attending no school was considered unimportant in 80 per cent of the cases. The last day attended was also considered so unimportant that it was omitted in 224 or 26 per cent of the reports. The school saw no particular value in reporting the child's record of previous truancy in 80 per cent of the reports.

It was evident that no serious attempt had been made to get in touch with the parents by letter. The age of the child was omitted in 162 reports and the principal's signature, to indicate any responsibility of the principal's office, was lacking in 224 or 26 per cent of the cases.

The two outstanding omissions in the reports of the attendance officers were the absence of any information regarding the person from whom cause of absence was determined and the lack of any report on the date of the pupils' return.

In all the cities studied the record of the days lost by the child before return was not considered a necessary measure of attendance service to the extent that it was made a requirement before a case was declared closed.

Cumulative Absence Records.—Not one of the cities investigated had a complete cumulative record of the total absences of reported cases. City B had grouped together in a more or less haphazard manner reported absences of the different individuals for whom a number of reports had come in and who appeared to be possible court cases, but they were kept for the current year only and constituted neither an accurate nor a complete record. In City K there was an endeavor to form such a record. The absence reports were filed alphabetically for each child. They were summarized during the summer for the preceding school year. Little use was made of them except for the annual report, in which the data gave the following history of truancy during the year.

CITY K—TRUANTS

Reported once.............................. 1963 cases
Reported twice............................. 471 cases
Reported three times....................... 184 cases
Reported four times........................ 96 cases
Reported 8 or more times................... 12 cases

TABLE X

DISTRIBUTION OF INFORMATION NOT GIVEN BY SCHOOLS AND ATTENDANCE
OFFICERS, AS FOUND IN 861 ABSENCE REPORTS

Information from Schools	*No. Lacking Information*		*Total*	*Per Cent*
	City D	*City E*		
1. No. of report...............	473	1	474	55.05
2. Name or No. of school......	21	1	22	2.56
3. Parent's name...............	71	109	180	20.91
4. Address	..	2	2	.23
5. Absent, truant, attending no school	394	298	692	80.37
6. Last day attended...........	86	138	224	26.05
7. Absent preceding week......	330	261	591	68.65
8. Times truant this term......	406	290	696	80.84
9. Parents written to...........	421	341	762	88.50
10. Remarks	218	118	336	39.02
11. Principal's signature........	220	4	224	26.02
12. Teacher's signature.........	10	98	108	12.56
13. Date	31	4	35	4.07
14. Age	42	120	162	18.82
15. Grade	7	5	12	1.35

REVERSE OF CARD

Attendance Officers' Report				
1. Investigation completed......	227	4	231	26.83
2. Interviewed Father, Mother.	425	108	533	61.90
3. Reported to Principal.......	116	9	125	14.52
4. Pupil returned to school.....	102	224	346	40.19
5. Causes of absence..........	43	3	46	5.34
6. Signature	14	..	14	1.61
7. Remarks	205	..	205	23.81

A somewhat similar system was employed in City N, but the individual reports were filed by months so that it was necessary to go through each month's file and collect the cards for any particular individual records to be investigated. The record of absences and final disposition would even then be incomplete.

In City G the cumulative record was incomplete and of no value in determining the time and extent of a pupil's absence record.

From the 487 individual records we were able to determine the number of times the individual records were reported during a period of five years. The attendance service had available the action taken in each case and in some instances the number of days' absence, but a complete record of total days' absence was for the most part lacking. Table XI shows one phase of the attendance problem in this city:

TABLE XI

DISTRIBUTION OF NUMBER OF REPORTS FOR 487 PUPILS

CITY J—1920-1925

Times Reported	Number of Pupils	Per Cent of Total
I	315	64.0
2	59	12.0
3	40	8.4
4	19	4.9
5	9	1.9
6	10	2.1
7	6	1.3
8	5	1.0
9	2	.4
10-15	14	2.9
15-20	5	1.0
Over 20	3	.6
Total	487	100.0

Such analyses give little indication of the real problem. The number of days illegally absent and the classification of truants by physical and economic conditions, scholarship, age and grade [2] are all lacking.

In City I a cumulative record showing the number of visits made to the homes out of 152 cases investigated was given in this form:

TABLE XII

DISTRIBUTION OF VISITS, CITY I

Number of Cases	Number of Visits
74	1st
29	2nd
16	3rd
10	4th
8	5th
4	6th
2	7th
2	8th
2	9th
1 each	10th, 11th, 12th, 13th, 14th

[2] Snedden, D. and Allen, W. H., *School Reports and School Efficiency*, p. 24.

The cumulative records found were for annual report purposes only. They are the traditional measures of the attendance officer's work. That these cases were reported repeatedly by the schools showed at least a determination on the part of the school to keep the attendance department informed as to the necessity for action in spite of the apparent inability of the attendance service to apply remedial measures. Instead of such records we should have available a complete case study giving the analytical method of treating the cases and the endeavor made to handle them intelligently and effectively. The new standard is a thorough study of the causes underlying every case referred to the department, with the idea of eliminating permanently the most difficult ones.

Transfers.—With our rapidly shifting population brought about by the complexities of modern, social, economic and industrial conditions, changes from one school to another, both between schools of the same city and those of other cities, are a source of serious educational loss. We may differentiate these changes or transfers into three types:

1. From and to classes in the same school.
2. From and to schools in the same city.
3. From and to schools in different cities or communities.

Such changes bring some serious problems to the attendance service:

1. To prevent any loss of school time in going from one school to the other, either public or non-public.
2. To make the necessary corrections, changes of address and school attended in the census report.
3. To prevent loss of school standing by the child being placed in a grade lower than the one of which he was a member at the transferring school.
4. To prevent loss of school records which form so important a part of the child's educational history.
5. To prevent loss of the attendance officer's time.

From the available transfer records, incomplete as they usually are, there is no difficulty in finding satisfactory evidence that many cases of truancy and illegal non-attendance are prevalent. In fact the general *laissez faire* attitude towards the transfer, its loss in time, school status and records is a contributing cause to the present conditions.

The loss brought about by the first type of transfer is negligible and is a responsibility which demands the assistance of the attendance service only when illegal non-attendance results from a recalcitrant attitude on the part of pupil or parent toward such transfer. These cases are comparatively few in number and require, as a rule, only the tactful approach to the problem to bring about a satisfactory adjustment. When immediate results are not forthcoming the attendance service can wisely but firmly force attendance.

The second type of transfers, "from and to schools of the same city," involves at the present time three kinds:

  a. From and to public schools.
  b. From and to public and non-public schools.
  c. From and to non-public schools.

In City D we find, by a sampling study of 206 transfers, the loss of school days as follows:

TABLE XIII
DISTRIBUTION OF TIME LOST IN TRANSFERS, CITY D

Days Lost	*Cases*	*Per Cent*
0	118	57.4
1	28	13.6
2	24	11.7
3	14	6.8
4	5	2.4
5 to 10	10	4.8
10 to 20	4	1.9
1 month	3	1.4
Total	206	100.0

No complete records of transfers were obtainable at the attendance office, but 160 teachers were asked to give the loss of time by transfer of pupils in their classes during the present year. Out of 3,579 transfers during the year 1923–24 only 72 cases were reported to the attendance department for investigation. From the above random sampling it is clearly evident that the loss of time in City D is a problem that is worthy of more consideration.

In City E we found, from a study of 700 transfer forms, the loss as follows:

TABLE XIV
Distribution of Time Lost in Transfers, City E

Days Lost	Cases	Per Cent
0	581	81.2
1	27	3.8
2	26	3.6
3	18	2.5
4	11	1.6
10 or more	5	.7
Dated ahead	48	6.7
Total	716	

In this city every transfer was supposed to be reported to the attendance department. The difference in percentages of loss in City D, where a very small percentage of cases is reported, and in City E, where all are reported, is evidenced in every group.

In the 716 transfer forms examined in City E, it was found that 48 were dated after the child was enrolled in the new school. The attendance officer on going to the homes to check up losses in enrollment found that many of the absentees had gone to work, left school because of the compulsory age limit, or were attending non-public schools. Nineteen of the cases found were attending parochial schools. The officer then compelled the child to return to the school last attended and secure a transfer to the new school. The teacher or principal of the former school, instead of dating the transfer as of the last day attended, dated it as of the day the transfer was requested. That the attendance department should be compelled to investigate so many cases of transfer within its own city schools showed a serious lack of coöperation and consideration of the child accounting requirements which are a necessity in a school system.

Loss of Grade Through Transfers.—The loss of school standing by the child due to transfers is not known, and no records are available. In the cities visited, however, one had recently had a conference of principals because of the complaint that all the schools in the city did not accept the record of pupils transferred and assigned pupils to a lower grade than the one recommended. The complaint was general that non-public schools did not grant full credit for public school records.

"There is conclusive evidence," says Ayres, "to show that pupils are retarded in their progress by transfers from one school to another. In the New York investigation the records showed 25 per cent more transfers among the retarded children than among the non-retarded children. It is manifest that children are bound to suffer more or less when they leave one school to attend another. In our shifting population such changes are so frequent as to effect a considerable part of the children attending school. It is the manifest duty of school superintendents, principals and teachers to see to it that just as often as possible the child who transfers from school to school shall proceed to his new class from the point at which he left his studies in the old one. In all such cases it is the child and not the school which should be given the benefit of the doubt." [3]

Loss of Record.—So far as the writer is aware no study has been made of the loss of school records due to transfers. That there should be a serious loss brought about by the present carelessness seems inevitable. A study was made in City D to obtain some objective evidence of what this loss might be. The data were obtained from the permanent records of 2,949 pupils in 96 classes from all grades (from 1 to 8). Table XV shows the grade records lost and the source of transfer. In 192 cases no record of the

TABLE XV

Loss of School Records by Transfer

2,949 Records—City D

1924-25

GRADE RECORDS LOST								SCHOOL FROM WHICH CHILD WAS TRANSFERRED					
1	2	3	4	5	6	7	8	Local	Foreign	Same state	Other state	Parochial	No record
35	24	17	14	11	4	0	0	0	4	5	2	2	22
16	13	9	7	5	2	1	..	..	3	2	2	..	9
57	47	31	11	5	3	..	..	2	8	8	10	13	15
34	26	20	12	8	5	3	2	2	4	8	4	2	14
35	25	18	7	1	..	..	..	2	3	6	3	7	14
34	23	14	5	..	..	..	..	..	3	..	..	1	31
35	26	18	12	3	2	..	..	..	..	..	..	..	35
41	34	18	11	5	1	..	..	7	3	3	4	10	14
36	31	18	15	9	4	2	..	1	1	..	..	7	27
7	2	..	..	..	..	..	..	..	..	1	1	1	4
30	21	13	5	2	..	..	..	1	8	5	8	7	1
33	13	8	5	3	..	..	..	4	5	6	5	2	11
Total 393	285	184	104	52	21	6	2	19	42	44	39	52	197
Per Cent. 13.4	9.7	6.3	3.5	1.8	.7	.2	.07	4.9	10.5	11.3	9.9	13.3	50.1

[3] Ayres, L. P., *Laggards in Our Schools*, p. 198.

previous school was found, but the facts discovered indicate that if a continuous school record is of any value the school to which the child is transferred should have made more of an effort to get the child's record of his previous schooling.

In each case where a grade record was lost all the preceding grade records were missing. Out of 104 pupils who had no fourth grade record, the first, second and third grade records were also missing. For this condition the local public and non-public schools were responsible for 18.2 per cent and cities in the same state for 11.3 per cent. Out of the 96 classes studied 86 had one or more pupils with lost records. In one sixth grade class seven pupils, or 18 per cent of the class had no records of previous schools attended. All had been transferred from other cities of the same state. Only seven classes had pupils without loss in complete records.

Responsibility for Transfers.—With the possibilities for loss of school time, records and school status, as well as the loss of the officer's time in investigating pupils lost in transfer, we may well examine into the responsibility for transfers and to whom this responsibility is entrusted. In Cities A, L, and E the attendance department is notified of all transfers and waits from three to ten days for notice from the receiving school that the pupil had been admitted before making any investigation. In all the other cities the department awaits a call from one or the other of the schools involved before investigating any delay.

Cities A, B, D, and E use duplicate forms, while Cities E, F, I, and M use a single card report to the admitting school. Cities N and O use telephone service entirely between the two schools and City L employs a five-part form in notifying the attendance officer and the admitting school and in checking and completing the transfer. All cities reported very little coöperation between public and non-public schools in the safeguarding of transfer.

In three cities, A, E, and L, the attendance department assumed direct responsibility in the case of transfers. In all other cities no serious loss was considered probable and the responsibility was left to the individual school and the superintendent.

In City C the child was expected to go to the superintendent's office for the transfer. If he could not come, the card was signed by the superintendent and sent to the admitting school, a duplicate being retained at the superintendent's office. There was no record to show the time lost before the child entered the new school. By personal inquiry of all records available (26 cases), it was found that the greatest loss was four days and that 18 days were lost in all.

The form in use will not of itself prevent the serious losses due to transfers. Each agency involved must be thoroughly appreciative of its responsibility in the matter. Upon the attendance department, however, rests the duty of immediately checking any failure in the completion of a transfer. The official time allowed to elapse between the issuance of the original "Notice of Transfer" and the "receipt" of the form by the attendance office denoting the child's admission varies from three to ten days. In City L it was possible to determine the actual practice. In this city where a five-part form was used there were 57 of the No. 1 blanks awaiting the receipt of blank No. 5 from the receiving school showing that the child had been admitted. An examination of these blanks disclosed the actual number of days that had elapsed since the child had been transferred without the attendance department taking any action to find out the reason for the delay.

TABLE XVI

DISTRIBUTION OF NUMBER OF SCHOOL DAYS ATTENDANCE DEPARTMENT HAD
WAITED FOR THE RECEIPT OF BLANK TO DENOTE A
COMPLETE TRANSFER

School Days	Number of Cases
4	2
5	10
6	13
7	1
8	4
9	1
10-15	14
20-24	12
Total	57

In the cases already closed no effort had been made to check the amount of time lost in transfers or to render such a study possible.

Although an effort was made to study the entire file the writer was allowed to study only those collected and arranged by the attendance clerk. There was every belief on the part of the school authorities that there was practically no loss in school time due to

TABLE XVII

DISTRIBUTION OF TIME LOST IN TRANSFER

CITY L—1924-25

School Days Lost	Number of Cases	Per Cent
0	123	42.0
1	74	26.0
2	43	14.5
3	24	8.1
4	7	2.2
5	8	2.3
6	6	2.1
7	6	2.1
9	1	.3
10	1	.3
30	1	.3
	294	100.0 [5]

[5] Only a portion of the entire number could be obtained. Those given were selected by attendance clerk.

transfers, since the principal of the transferring school always telephoned to the school to which transfer was to be made in order to avoid any loss of time.

As a number of these transfers were for the continuation school where the child was compelled to report for but one day each week, fifty of these transfers were taken out and studied separately. The record for continuation school transfers is shown in the following table.

TABLE XVIII

DISTRIBUTION OF SCHOOL DAYS LOST IN TRANSFER TO THE CONTINUATION SCHOOL

CITY L—1924-25

School Days Lost	Number of Cases
0	13
1	5
2	4
3	2
4	4
5	5
10-15	4
20-30	2
31	1
5 months	1
Total	43 [6]

[6] NOTE.—In five cases the transfers for both schools were dated by the transferring school. In three cases the date of receiving transfers was from one to six days prior to date to transfer.

DISMISSALS

When a school drops the name of a pupil from the school enrollment for a more or less permanent period, it is called a dismissal, withdrawal, left, or discharge. Transfers from one school to another school of the same school system or to a school of another city, when finally closed, constitutes a discharge or dismissal, as do the more generally accepted causes for such action:

1. Death of pupil.
2. Removal of pupil from district.
3. Legal employment.
4. Withdrawal after completing compulsory age period.
5. Physician's certificate for mental or physical inability to attend school.
6. Not found.
7. Marriage.

One of the most important contributing factors to inefficient attendance service is the practice found in many cities of discharging, dismissing, or dropping pupils from the school roll without full authorization from the attendance department. When an effort is being made to maintain a continuing census and an efficient system of child accounting such action means a decentralization of authority that is a handicap to a proper administration of attendance service and often results in serious loss of school attendance. Since 1862 when the Chicago rule allowing a child's name to be dropped from the roll at the end of five days' absence was more or less generally adopted, the "temporary left" practice has been employed in many cities, openly or secretly, to maintain a high per cent of attendance. Moehlman estimates that the difference between the use of the "temporary left" rule and accurate accounting is approximately ten per cent.[7]

While per cent of attendance was the only measure of attendance used the practice became general. Names were dropped from the roll after five days' absence and in some places after three days' absence. Those dropped were, at times, considered as "left" from the beginning of the absence period. Many variations of the "Chicago Rule" are now in practice. Out of 233 registers and

[7] Moehlman, A. B., *Child Accounting*, p. 21.

state forms 23 gave definite rules for determining membership. Of this number five dropped pupils from the roll after three days' absence, six after five days' absence, three after ten days' absence, one after four weeks' absence and the remaining eight retained pupils as members until dropped for legal exemption.[8]

The cities reporting their practice show even greater variation.

Dropping Pupils from Roll.[9]—The cities studied did not officially countenance the practice but acknowledged that it was being done by some schools in order to raise the per cent of attendance —the only measure commonly used by school authorities to determine the efficiency of attendance service.

In a recent state bulletin we find the statement, "An effort was made to compare school attendance facts with other states in the Union, but the available figures of many of the states are not comparable with our figures owing to their variable rules governing the recording of attendance in the school registers. This state records pupils as either present or absent after enrollment until the end of the school year, except in cases of death or removal from the district, while in many of the other states a pupil absent three or five days is considered off roll to avoid credit for absence which results in increasing the percentage of attendance in those states."

Official belief does not always square with actual practice. In Cities D, E, F, G, and H of the state referred to above pupils were "dropped from roll" when the absence continued for a week or longer, the time being left to the individual school. The overemphasis placed upon a high percentage rating and the ranking of all cities in the state by the state authorities on this basis is often too great a temptation. To avoid carrying a habitual truant or continued absence for other reasons, a child was temporarily dropped from roll. City O was the only city in which such practice was denied.

State regulations regarding enrollment have been issued by some states to prevent a practice that has been widespread and pernicious. Pennsylvania, in 1920, made it obligatory that "no child shall be counted as not belonging to the school unless, upon investigation by the local attendance bureau or the proper official, it shall be

[8] Heck, A. O., in *Educational Research Bulletin*, Oct. 29, 1924, p. 299.
[9] Bermejo, F. V., *School Attendance Service in American Cities*, p. 113.

found that the child is (*a*) deceased, (*b*) has moved from district, (*c*) is enrolled in another school, (*d*) is legally employed, (*e*) is 16 years of age and withdrawn from school, (*f*) has been certified by medical inspector as incapacitated, (*g*) or excused by the superintendent for legal reasons." [10]

In 1921 the "Intercity Conference" made as one of its two definite contributions that temporary lefts and withdrawals be discontinued and "that a pupil is to be considered as a member of a school until he is known to have been permanently discharged by reason of death, removal from the district, or discharged as a result of having fulfilled the requirements of the compulsory education law." [11]

In City D the attendance department received 70 discharges or lefts on November 25 for pupils transferred to other school systems. The lists when received comprised discharges of the following dates:

Month	Number of Discharges or Lefts
June, 1924	39
Sept., 1924	12
Oct., 1924	12
Nov., 1924	16

In the same city 17 discharge blanks were found on December 2 enclosed in the September 30 reports of change of address which had not been reported on the census cards. Over three months had elapsed since the pupil had left the local school and no inquiry had gone out to the receiving school to prevent loss of educational opportunities during the interim or to determine actual cause of leaving. No one in the transferring city knew whether these pupils were in school or not. Had the attendance officer alone had the power to discharge a pupil, the transferring school, after waiting a reasonable length of time, would have asked for permission to drop from roll the names of the pupils transferred rather than continue to lose in the per cent of attendance.

Even when these transfer or dismissal forms are sent out to other cities with a request for a reply as to the enrollment of the pupil, there is apparently little or no general appreciation on the part of school authorities that it is a responsibility and a duty, if not a courtesy, to reply.

[10] *Digest of Laws Controlling School Attendance,* Department of Public Instruction, Pennsylvania, 1922, pp. 7-8.
[11] Moehlman, E. H., *Child Accounting,* p. 177.

A study of 682 cases showed the following conditions :

City	Discharge Blanks Sent Out	Replies Received	No Replies	Per Cent Replies
D	154	77	77	50
E	528	251	277	47
Total	682	328	328	

Cities D and E had kept a record of their dismissals and replies. From this it is seen that of the notices sent out, approximately 50 per cent of the attendance departments considered it worth while to reply.

In one city only, City D, was it possible to make a study of 67 discharge blanks to other cities with return slips from the receiving school giving the time of arrival of the transferred pupil. These return slips showed six cases in which no date was given for the enrollment in the receiving school, and 47 gave information as to the time intervening between discharge and admission to the new school. Table XIX shows the loss of time.

TABLE XIX

DISTRIBUTION OF 47 TRANSFERS TO OTHER CITIES

CITY D

Cases	Days Lost
10	0
6	1
9	2
5	3
1	4
4	5
3	6
5	8
1	9
1	10
1	11
1	24

That many of the schools often date the transfer or dismissal not at the actual time of the transfer but at the time the case may be brought officially or otherwise to their attention, is shown by the fact that 14 of the 67 cases were dated as transferred from 1 to 63 days after the child had been enrolled in the other school. In Cities B, F, C, I, L, M, N, and O the attendance department did little or nothing to supervise dismissals. The matter was left

with the individual schools. Cities A, G, H, D, J, and E sent
notices, but only Cities A, H, and E expected replies that the child
had enrolled. City K merely verified the report that the child had
left the city when the school reported a lack of information as to
where the child had gone. Cities D and E, however, followed up
the first inquiry by a second and a third if necessary. Even such
measures brought only partial returns.

In all the cities a lack of strict supervision of those who left
school constituted a source of continued annoyance and loss.
Public or non-public schools not held in strict accountability for all
those leaving were opening the way for employment without legal
certificates and for a group of non-attendants who might be discovered by chance contact with the attendance department.

Measuring Regularity of Attendance.—The regularity of attendance is generally presented in one or even more of the following
methods:

1. By comparing the number being instructed with the number on roll at the time.
2. By comparing the number of children present with the
   entire number on roll during the year.
3. By comparing the aggregate number of days attended with
   the total possible days attended.
4. By comparing the aggregate number of days attended with
   the aggregate number of days belonging.
5. By recording the actual number of days each child attended
   and tabulating the results in periods from one to nine
   days, ten to nineteen days, etc., up to the total length of
   the school term.

By the use of the first method, the dropping of pupils from the
roll, insures a high percentage, but this figure has little if any
significance. The second method, though more truly informational
than the first, does not tell the number of children who reported
regularly or how many had frequent absences.

The third method was used in Cities D, E, F, G, and H and is
subject to the same weakness as the first, if pupils are dropped
from the roll without legal exemption. Even where they are not
dropped, the transferred pupils were not counted absent during the
days lost in transfer and the total possible days of attendance was

reduced, thereby resulting in a fictitious percentage. Children not reporting at the beginning of the term were not on roll and the possible days of attendance were thus reduced.

The fourth method was used in Cities N and O. As the state law prevented "dropping from the roll" except for legal exemptions, it should give the same result as the third method if terms were accurately defined. Neither method offers a true analysis of attendance conditions.

Not one of the cities showed the number of children on the basis of actual number of days attended. Such a record gives most valuable information for determining the regularity of attendance, but even it may conceal the true conditions, if, as in City L, the school registers are closed two weeks before the end of the school term and the attendance for the last week is made a duplication of the two weeks preceding the closing of the registers.

As long as certain percentage standards of attendance are sought or expected, some school will make every effort to attain them. What is desired is a statement of real facts upon which to determine the actual conditions of attendance and to apply the remedial measures where they are required.

City I, endeavoring to avoid the use of percentage in comparing attendance conditions in the different schools, deducted all absence for personal illness or illness in the family except where illness was excessive, and regarded all others as unnecessary absences. The registration was divided into the times absent, thus giving the times absent per capita. Such a report is shown below:

School	*No. Registered Between 7 and 16*	*Times Absent*	*Times Absent per Capita*
I	419	95	.2267
2	146	76	.5205
3	425	402	.9458
4	198	240	1.2120

This was used as a basis of comparison of schools but the deductions made were so arbitrary that it showed only a partial condition of the attendance.

By such a report some schools were often shown with low records because of religious holidays although the actual attendance was more carefully safeguarded than in schools with better official records. The attendance problem cannot be solved en masse. It is an individual problem and the records used should offer help in locating the problem and securing the necessary remedial measures.

SUMMARY OF PROBLEMS OF ATTENDANCE SERVICE

From the foregoing discussion of the conditions underlying the problem of city school attendance service, we have endeavored to analyze three phases of the problem, absences, transfers, and dismissals. There is evidence of a lack of uniformity in the methods of reporting absence, ranging from the use of the telephone, the mail, the awaiting of the personal call of the attendance officer, to no report at all. In no case was there a feeling that the attendance service was adequate to cope with the non-attendance that should be investigated. The schools, for the most part, referred to the attendance department only that portion of cases which experience showed that the department could handle. Information from the schools was incomplete and addresses inaccurate, often resulting in serious loss of time on the part of the attendance officer.

In all cities the absence allowed before a case was reported was apparently determined by the capacity of the department. In no city studied was an immediate reporting of all unexcused absences expected or called for. The attendance department had no adequate records of the actual results of their service. More or less futile attempts were made by two cities to have records of practical value, but the practice prevailed of meeting each case independently of any known previous record.

Frequency of visits and number of cases investigated, rather than the illegal days absent, were considered the measures of service rendered. The two most important agencies of attendance service, the school and the attendance department, were not so coördinated in their efforts that the one fully knew what the other was attempting to do or had accomplished.

There appeared to be no lack of earnest endeavor but there always prevailed a spirit of resignation to a task which an inadequate staff rendered beyond their power.

Lack of administrative standards and an unwarranted variation in the investigation and treatment of cases were noticeable.

The emphasis of police function was growing less prevalent, but an insufficient staff made a case study of the absentees too limited to form an important part of the attendance service.

We have seen that the transfer problem involved irregularity of attendance, loss of time, school, grade and records. This appears particularly true of transfers to and from public and non-public schools. There was slackness in dating transfers, as shown in City E where 48 were dated as admitted from 10 to 20 days before the child was actually transferred. Eighteen of these were to parochial schools. Names were often changed when a child entered a non-public school and this brought new difficulties of investigation.

The form of transfers ranged from the simplest one-card type like that of City C to a five-part form with (*a*) Notice of discharge, (*b*) Discharge for transfer, (*c*) Notice of discharge for transfer, (*d*) Acknowledgment of transfer, and (*e*) Notice of admission by transfer, whereby the discharging and receiving schools and the attendance department were expected to follow the course of the transfer and prevent delay.

The attitude towards permanent or temporary dismissals, "lefts," or withdrawals of pupils is a source of serious weakness in attendance service. Comparison of attendance of different cities becomes fictitious. Records are inaccurate and loss of attendance far-reaching.

There is not yet a full realization that attendance service is for all the children regardless of the kind of school attended. With no uniformity in the methods of measuring the regularity of attendance on a percentage basis, or a true analysis of attendance on a basis of actual days attended, little comparable information is available.

POLICIES OF ATTENDANCE SERVICE IN SECURING REGULARITY
OF ATTENDANCE

Certain policies of attendance service must form the background of any plan of organization and administration for securing regularity of attendance. These policies must correctly interpret the requirements of the statutes and the community ideals of school attendance.

In setting up the methods to meet the problem as we have seen it in the light of the cities studied, the following standards of attainment should form the basis of effective service in any city:

1. That every child of compulsory school age should attend school every day unless legally excused.
2. That the absence of every child for which the school has no legal excuse should be investigated at once.
3. That no child once enrolled in the schools, public or non-public, should be lost from the school enrollment without full knowledge of the attendance department.
4. That the record of the legal and illegal absences of all pupils of all schools, public and non-public, should be available.
5. That there shall be, at all times, constant, accurate and complete accounting of all attendance service offered by all agencies of the school authorities.

FORMS AND RECORDS RECOMMENDED

Form 23. Teacher's Register or Classroom Record.
" 24. Individual Record of Attendance.
" 25. Report of Non-Attendance.
" 26. School Record of Non-Attendance Reports.
" 27. Principal's Summary of Non-Attendance Reports.
" 28. Monthly Report of Principal to Superintendent.
" 29. Cumulative Absence Record for Attendance Department.
" 30. Report of Incompleted Investigations.
" 31. Directions for Use of Non-Attendance Reports.
" 32. Notice of Transfers.
" 33. Memorandum of Transferred Record.
" 34. Admission, Discharge and Promotion Card.
" 35. Attendance Office Record of Non-Attendance Cases Assigned to Attendance Officer.
" 36. Daily Report of Attendance Officer.
" 37. Monthly Report of Attendance Officer.
" 38. Monthly Report of Attendance Office to Superintendent of Schools.
" 39 Annual Report of Attendance Office to Superintendent of Schools.
" 40. Absence-Age-Grade Table.

Form 41. Monthly Grade-Report of Entries, Withdrawals and Attendance.
" 42. Monthly School Summary of Entries, Withdrawals and Attendance.
" 43. Monthly City Summary of Entries, Withdrawals and Attendance.
" 44. Annual City Summary of Entries, Withdrawals and Attendance.

Many other forms may be used in accordance with the size and community ideals of attendance service to be rendered. The above forms and reports are, however, essential for securing full regularity of attendance. The forms already described in the previous chapter are of necessity a basis for knowing where the child is. This enables the attendance service to secure enrollment without loss of attendance.

DESCRIPTION OF FORMS, RECORDS AND PROCEDURE RECOMMENDED

The city should be divided into attendance districts of one or more school districts, equalized as nearly as possible in area to be covered, school population and the difficulty of district due to character and number of cases to be investigated. Experience will show that the number of investigations of census and attendance cases will make readjustments necessary on the basis of work to be done. These districts should be coterminus with the regular census districts, making it possible for the attendance officer to become personally acquainted with his district and to know and to be known by the parents and children.

Experience shows that problems of non-attendance and juvenile delinquency are often adjusted by a better understanding between home and school. These adjustments must be made by the attendance officer whenever possible, and it is by his thorough knowledge of his district that he is able to reach the real causes underlying non-attendance and truancy. The coöperation of parents must be enlisted and compulsion held in the background for cases that cannot be handled otherwise. The right kind of help for one child often changes the attitude of a home towards the school and makes possible the better attendance of the other children in the family. The attendance officer is not merely an officer of the law, walking his beat, but a friend seeking the means of enabling the school to do as much as possible for the child.

The officer upon his daily report to the central office, or to the district office in the larger cities, may receive emergency cases from any school in his district before leaving for the schools to be visited. These cases should be recorded by the clerk by consecutive school number and case number on the daily office record of non-attendance reports. A regular program must be followed and each school visited each day unless experience shows the number of cases do not justify daily visits. This will be particularly true of non-public schools until they look to the attendance officer for a service similar to that of the public schools.

In City E, 916 visits were made to non-public schools and 117 cases were reported to the attendance officers. The waste of time in making such visits should be avoided. The report showed that in some instances an officer visited a school every day for a month without receiving a case for investigation. A telephone call to such a school would avoid this loss of time. The program of the officer must be so well known and definite that he can be reached by the central office or by any school of his district for emergency or other investigations for both morning and afternoon sessions. In cases that had been assigned to him by telephone, the "non-attendance report" of the school can later be completed upon his next visit to the school. The office record must show such assignments and his daily report will complete the office record.

Cities do not yet fully appreciate the value of prompt action. An attendance officer with adequate transportation can investigate as many cases as two officers.[12]

If, as recommended in Chapter II, the number of officers is based upon an organization of one officer for each 3,000 pupils of compulsory school age, the ratio may be reduced, the social case work developed and the productive character of the work of the attendance department raised by providing suitable transportation facilities.

Such a staff is not required for investigation of mere truancy cases, as the work in some cities is now administered. A modern attendance service requires the continuing enumerations and checking of census cases. Along with this must be prompt investigation

[12] Denver, Colo., Monograph No. 8, p. 13.

of all unexcused absence and the immediate adjustment of the child to a proper relationship with the school, thus saving the repetition of grades and the possible future costs of delinquency. For such service more time must be spent in contact with home and child rather than in the exercise of walking the streets.

Form 23. Teacher's Register or Classroom Record.—To make prompt investigation possible (*a*) the teacher must record immediately and accurately all absences in her classroom at the opening of each school session. State record forms or "registers" are usually provided for this purpose and determine the type of record to be kept. Her second duty (*b*) is to notify the principal of all absences and the reason known to her to be the cause of such absence.

The method of allowing teachers to determine the names that should be reported scatters the responsibility too widely and makes accountability for non-attendance difficult. The school principal is the person responsible for the administration of the school. It would be impractical and unnecessary to provide attendance officers to investigate every case of absence, but the attendance department must be held responsible and must be adequately staffed to provide immediate service for all cases for which the school does not know the cause and does not understand the type of service that is required, to meet the individual child.

The Teacher's Register or Classroom Record, in which are recorded all entries, withdrawals, absences and tardiness together with periodic summary of all attendance data, is the original source of all attendance information required either by state or by local authorities. Many states now furnish the required forms and these no doubt must be continued until authority is found by which greater national uniformity may be secured.

Lack of detailed instructions in the use of the forms and ambiguity in the interpretation of the terms are the source of much of the indefinite information now prevailing in attendance figures. In one state visited the registers are sent to the state department, where the totals are checked and the registers returned to the district only to be laid aside. As a permanent record their value is seldom recognized. In only one attendance office, City I, were these registers of the previous year arranged for easy accessibility and use.

Form 24.   Individual Record of Attendance.—To supply the data on attendance needed for the proper enforcement of the compulsory education law a loose-leaf or card form should be provided for each child on the register.   This becomes the cumulative attendance record of the child for the use of the attendance service.   It must be a correct up-to-date transcript of the class register, and when a child is absent it becomes the teacher's "non-attendance or absence report" to the principal.   In form and content it should be the same as the "absent report" (Form 25).   Upon the return of the child to school this record is returned to the teacher with report of action taken in the case.

Form 25.   Report of Non-Attendance.—As soon as possible after the opening of each school session the teacher must send the cumulative attendance record of each absent pupil to the office of the principal.   From these reports the principal or person delegated to this work must determine those who require investigation by the attendance department.   All cases of suspected truancy, unexcused absences, and absences where there may be need of assistance of any kind should be reported.

The absence report blank is then filled out by the school office giving the officer the cumulative record of all cases reported and the information that will make it possible for him to render intelligent service.   The child is being brought to the attention of the "absence hospital" and only when all the symptoms and full run of the disease are available for investigation can the department adequately diagnose the case and prescribe the most effective treatment.   In such cases a full transcript of the year's attendance is necessary, showing month and days of absence with the school summary for each report that has been sent, together with special information or comment for each report made.

The blank should be a two-page form giving the following items:

1. Name of child
2. Date of birth, grade and room
3. Name of parent or guardian, teacher's name
4. Telephone number
5. Where employed
6. Number of the report
7. Sessions absent for each report—
   a. Excused, *b.* Unexcused, *c.* Total
8. Date of report

9. Date of investigation
10. Probable return
11. Date of return
12. Result of investigation—
    a. Drop name
    b. Lawful absence, number and cause
    c. Unlawful absence
13. Special case action
14. Officer's name

FORM 25. REPORT OF NON-ATTENDANCE

Report of Non-Attendance	City of...........................

Last name First name B G Parent or guardian
....
Phone......... Where employed...................
Present address............... ....School......Grade......Room.....
....
Teacher................... Birth, Mo.....Day.....Yr...........

Report of Sessions Absent, year.....
Check date of absence, Code-Whole day V;A.M. ;P.M. ;D.Dropped;
Re.Re-entered.

Date	1	2	3	4	5	— — — — — — — — — — — — — — —	27	28	29	30	31
Sept.											
Oct.											
Nov.											
Dec.											
June											

Report of Absence   Date of

No.	School		Officer		Lawful		Unlawful		Re-	Inves- tiga- tion	Prob- able ret'n	Re- turn'd	Spec- ial action	Office name
	Ex- cus- ed	Unex- cus- ed	To- tal	Drop name	No.	Cause	No.	Cause	port					

On the reverse side of the card should be given all detailed information from the school to the officer and from the officer to the school after completion of investigation. This information should be given with the number and date of report to which it applies.

[Reverse of Form 25]

Report	Comments of School	Comments of Attendance Officer
1	....	....
2	....--..	....
3	....	....
9	....	....
10	....	....

Date		Report: Reason for Dismissal
Mo.	Day.	School _____ Officer
		School _____ Officer
		School _____ Officer

The attendance department should not only return the child to the school without delay, but it should also furnish the teacher with the reasons discovered for the absence as well as the treatment offered. Without such information the school and the attendance department could not have unity of effort, and at times they would even be working at cross purposes. To furnish this information in detail in all cases of absences reported would necessitate an unjustifiable amount of clerical work on the part of the teacher and the department. To obviate much of this difficulty and still give both the school and the department an adequate working basis for its remedial efforts, a code should be employed giving the causes of absence and the treatment offered. Letters A, B, C, D, with numerical subdivisions, as A 1, B 1, or a numerical code, as I 1, II 1, should be used.

The four most important divisions for attendance reports as to distribution of cases should be, Drop Name, Lawful, Unlawful, and Special Action. A code for such a record could be:

A. Drop Name	B. Lawful	C. Unlawful	D. Special Action
A 1 Transferred	B 1 Illness of	C 1 Truancy	D 1 Notice to
A 2 Incapaci-	child	C 2 Parents	parent
tated	B 2 Parent	C 3 Illegally em-	D 2 Interview
A 3 Not found	B 3 Death in	ployed	D 3 Examination
A 4 Legally em-	family	C 4 Other un-	D 4 Mental ex-
ployed	B 4 Poverty	lawful rea-	amination
A 5 Left city	B 5 Quarantine	son	D 5 Social
A 6 Dead	B 6 Court		Agency
A 7 Other rea-	B 7 Other rea-		D 6 Court
sons	sons		
A 8 Under com-			
pulsory age			

Care should be taken to render it possible to give further detail in D 5 and D 6 so that the school may be fully cognizant of the effort being made, and if possible coöperate with these agencies. The social agencies in different communities are so varied and changing that by coding all these agencies with a small letter, as D 5 a, D 5 b, etc., the teacher may know what particular agency of those listed in the "Direction Sheet" is endeavoring to bring about more satisfactory attendance for some child in her class. She will thus be able to participate more intelligently in the efforts being made.[13]

Form 26. School Record of Non-Attendance Reports.—In the principal's office in each school a loose-leaf record of all investigations should be kept. The cases for the school are numbered consecutively and entered in the book at the time they are turned over to the officer, or telephoned to him or to the central office. The code prescribed for the absence report should be used.

The form follows:

FORM 26. SCHOOL RECORD OF NON-ATTENDANCE REPORTS

ABSENCE INVESTIGATION				CITY OF						
SCHOOL NO.	CASE NO.	NAME	AD-DRESS	DATE OF REP'T	DATE OF RET'N	DROPPED	CAUSE		SPECIAL ACTION	REMARKS
							LAWFUL NO. CAUSE	UNLAWFUL NO. CAUSE		

Form 27. Principal's Summary of Non-Attendance Reports. —When made from day to day with carbon copy this may con-

[13] Nudd, H. W., Bureau of Compulsory Education, p. 10, and Department of Public Instruction, Penna. Bulletin, May, 1922.

stitute the school's monthly report to the attendance office. This is required to check the work of the attendance department and to give the date of return of all cases investigated. Principals have in the "Remark" column an opportunity to explain disapproval of action taken. The numbers may be consecutive for the year, thus giving the total investigations to date, or for any particular period. Any future reference can be made to this number and further details obtained from the individual non-attendance report. The case number is the number of the report for each individual and refers to a particular investigation of a child's non-attendance.

Form 28. Monthly Report of Principal to Superintendent.—In order that the superintendent of schools may have the school attendance service in terms of both that offered by the attendance department and that offered by the schools, a form should be used showing the distribution of all absences in accordance with the number of days absent and the disposition of the cases.

The report should also show the number of cases under each item which have been investigated by the school and by the attendance department. By this report the superintendent will be able to determine to what extent the school is assuming a responsibility of attendance, through the school nurse, the visiting nurse or otherwise, also the length of time required to close cases of any type.

This report will be especially helpful in cases of high schools, continuation schools, or other schools where the absence may be largely investigated by the school.

Form 28a. Suspense Register.—Both the school and the attendance department must maintain a Suspense Register or file of those who from temporary disability have been excused from school attendance in either public or non-public schools. Such registration by the school must be upon physician's certificate, as shown in Form 20, and filed in the Attendance Department by schools, with signals attached denoting date of probable return. The school on the monthly report (Form 28) gives the number on (*a*) Registration at the beginning of the month, (*b*) Placed on register during the month, (*c*) Removed from register during month, (*d*) On register at end of month. If found desirable, these figures may show the distribution by causes, such as quar-

FORM 28. MONTHLY ATTENDANCE REPORT OF PRINCIPAL

MONTHLY ATTENDANCE REPORT OF PRINCIPAL ----- CITY OF -----

SCHOOL ----- MONTH ENDING -----

DISTRIBUTION OF ABSENCE

DAYS ABS	A—DROPPED FROM ROLL									B—LAWFUL								C—UNLAWFUL					D—SPECIAL ACTION							TOTAL
	TOTAL	A1	A2	A3	A4	A5	A6	A7	A8	TOTAL	B1	B2	B3	B4	B5	B6	B7	TOTAL	C1	C2	C3	C4	TOTAL	D1	D2	D3	D4	D5	D6	
1—2																														
3—4																														
5—6																														
7—8																														
21—22																														
TOTAL																														
INVESTIGATED BY SCHOOL																														
INVESTIGATED BY AT. OF.																														
TOTAL																														
PERCENT																														

For the interpretation of Code Used (A1, A2), etc., see page 93.

1. Number of cases pending at beginning of month............
2. Number of new cases reported to attendance department............
3. Total cases of investigation............
4. Number of cases pending at close of month............
5. On suspense register at beginning of month............
6. Placed on suspense register during month............
7. Removed from suspense register during month............
8. On suspense register at end of month............

antine and temporary disability of less than 30 days, 60 days or 90 days.

A duplicate of this report should be sent to the attendance department to enable the department to know for what part of the attendance service it has been responsible.

Form 29. Cumulative Absence Record for Attendance Department.—The attendance department should have a complete Cumulative Absence Record of all cases treated, not only for reference and record but for a check upon the work of the attendance officers. Its content will be a transcript of the investigations of the non-attendance report. These records are filled out from the non-attendance reports by the clerk in the attendance office and filed alphabetically by schools for one month before being filed alphabetically in a general school file. These cards should be checked with the monthly reports of the school to the attendance department and the date of return of each absentee recorded.

FORM 29. CUMULATIVE ABSENCE RECORD

Cumulative Absence Record.	City of...														
Last name First name	B	G	Parent or Guardian												
Phone			Where employed												
Present Address			School.......Grade........Room....												
Teacher							Birth, Mo. Day Yr.							
	Report of Absence						Date of							
No	School				Officer				Inves tiga tion	Prob able ret'n	Re turn	Spec ial' action	Offi cer's Name
	Ex cus ed	Unex cus ed	To tal	Drop name	Lawful		Unlawful		Re port					
					No	Cause	No	Cause						
1														
2														
3														
4														
5														

[Reverse of Form 29]

Similar to Lower Half of Obverse

Date			Report: Reason for Dismissal.
Mo.	Day	School Officer	_____
		School Officer	_____

By being filed for the current month these records [14] can be compared with the school's monthly reports to the attendance department for date of return and final disposition of the case as recorded by the school. After the attendance officer has made his investigation it may be necessary for him in emergency cases to make a telephone report either direct from one school to another or through the central office. At the central office the history of the case is recorded on the cumulative office record of the reported absentees. The non-attendance report is returned to the school next day by the attendance officer, where the record is completed as to date of return.

In case further action or investigation is required the "incomplete absence report" (Form 30) is taken to the school in lieu of the absence report until a complete disposition of the case is made. The non-attendance reports for those who do not return on the date given by the officer must again be given to the officer until the child returns. The failure of the schools to do this can be noted from the monthly reports of the schools to the attendance department. Different colored forms may be used for boys and girls or for public and non-public schools.

Form 30. Report of Incomplete Investigations.—In case an attendance officer is unable to report the cause of absence and the probable date of return, a memorandum giving the school number and the case number, the name and address of the pupil and the cause of delay should be left with the principal the next day. It may take the following form:

FORM 30. REPORT OF INCOMPLETE INVESTIGATIONS

Memorandum of Cases Pending.			City of......................		
School & No.	Case No.	Name	Address	Reported	Reasons for delay in investigation
			Attendance Officer		

[14] See Form 75, Philadelphia Public Schools.

Form 31.   Directions for Use of Non-Attendance Reports.—
Definite printed instructions must be issued for the use of non-
attendance or absence reports.   Such instructions should be a part
of the form itself.

Absences.—The instructions must include directions for the
absences to be reported as determined by the school authorities.
Every unexcused absence should, however, be investigated at once
by the school or the attendance officer and the officer should be
provided with a transcript of the child's attendance record complete to date with other information that will aid him.

Dismissals and Withdrawals.—All pupils to be dropped from
the roll if previously reported should have their record completed,
with the cause of withdrawal given; otherwise no absence record
need be sent to the attendance department.

Transfers.—In case of transfer, the non-attendance report
should be made of the current year's attendance record of the
child and sent to the admitting school with the A. D. P. record and
Notice of Transfer.   A copy of the information code and directions for its use must be part of this form.

Form 32.   Notice of Transfers.—There may seem to be no
need for a particular method for making transfers, but it is necessary that the method used be enforced with thoroughness and zeal,
thus avoiding the losses that so often occur.   The quadruplicate
form on page 99 should be printed on carbonized paper, making it
possible to fill out all necessary items at one writing.   Number 1
should be mailed or sent at once to the attendance office.   Number 4 is retained by the principal of the transferring school as a
desk memorandum of an active case.   Number 2 is mailed or sent
by the attendance officer to the receiving school, and Number 3
is given to the child with his other school records (A. D. P. and
Non-Attendance Report) required by the receiving school to furnish the necessary school history.   The child presents Number 3
with his records for admission.   The receiving school then sends
Number 2 to the attendance officer, giving the date and half day
that the child entered.   The receipt of Number 2 is therefore a
notice of the completion of the transfer.   Number 3 is immediately returned to the transferring school and the case is then
closed for that school.

This form contains a place for certification that the full records

have been received. When this is not checked the attendance
office has the responsibility of following up the case not alone
for the local public and non-public schools but for the schools of
another city or community.

FORM 32. NOTICE OF TRANSFERS

NOTICE OF TRANSFER, ADMISSION, DISMISSAL.   City of...............

School.................... Date.......................... No.......

Name......................
Boy
Girl.....Birth Mo.....Day....Yr.....
last   first

Parent.....................Address No........St.................

Grade........ Room........ Teacher...........................

New Address No...........Street................................

School to which   School to which
transferred .... admitted ....

Admitted Mo......Day.....Yr...
A.M.
P.M.
Grade
assigned....
Records Yes
received No

(Signed)   Principal

Directions: Send Form 1 to Att. Dept. immediately. Give Form 2 to child. Send
Form 3 to school to which transfer is made. Retain Form 4 as memorandum.
Admitting school must send Form 2 to Att. Dept. and Form 3 to transferring school.

DIAGRAM OF ROUTINE FOR NOTICE OF TRANSFER

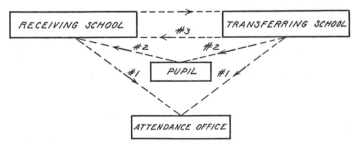

Although these forms should constitute a complete record of
the transfers and a check upon any delay or incompleteness, the
schools will find that telephone communication from one school
to another and to the attendance department will often avoid
special action by the attendance department.

Form 33. Memorandum of Transferred Record.—The following form will prove a helpful record when future inquiries may arise regarding any transferred child.

FORM 33. MEMORANDUM OF TRANSFERRED RECORD

MEMORANDUM OF TRANSFERRED RECORD. City of	
Transferred from.......................School	To be filled out whenever a pupil's permanent record is sent to another school and placed in alphabetical file of records of former pupil.
Transferred to..........................School	
Date of Transfer Grade at time of transfer	
Address at date of transfer	
Permanent record sent................By............................	
Receipt acknowledged by..	
Date of acknowledgment.......................Grade assigned......	

This form is also a permanent record of the transfer, showing completion and receipt of records.

Form 34. Admission, Discharge and Promotion Card.—It is important that the child's record of school progress should be transferred with the child from school to school within the city or to other schools when he changes his address to another city. For this purpose an Admission, Discharge, Promotion (A. D. P.) Card is now generally used. When leaving school permanently the child is permitted to retain it. The form recommended by the Committee on Uniform Records and Reports is adequate for this purpose. An adaptation of the contents of this card is shown below. It has one advantage—more spaces for changes of address.

The form of the record is shown on page 101.

Form 35. Attendance Office Record of Non-Attendance Cases Assigned to Attendance Officer.—A daily record should be kept in the central office of all cases assigned to the attendance officer by the schools or by the central office. Such a record will be somewhat similar to the record maintained by each school as shown in Form 26. The form should give the information below:

1. Consecutive number of the central office.
2. Consecutive school number of each case reported or the source of report.

FORM 34. ADMISSION, DISCHARGE AND PROMOTION CARD

Form 35 (*Continued*)

    3. Case number, as shown on the individual non-attendance report.
    4. Name and address of the absentee.
    5. Date of the report.
    6. Date of return.
    7. Cause for dropping name from roll.
    8. Number and cause of lawful and unlawful absences.
    9. Statement of "special action" of "case pending."
   10. Officer to whom case is assigned.

FORM 35. ATTENDANCE OFFICE RECORD OF NON-
ATTENDANCE CASES ASSIGNED AND
ATTENDANCE OFFICER

City of....................
Daily Report of Attendance Officer's Assignments
No.	Source or School No.	Case No.	Name	Address	Date of Rep't	Date of Ret'n	Dropped	Lawful		Unlawful		Special action	Name of Officer
								No	Cause	No	Cause		

FORM 36. DAILY REPORT OF ATTENDANCE OFFICER

DAILY REPORT OF ATTENDANCE OFFICER   CITY OF ____

NAME OF OFFICER   DATE OF REPORT

NUMBER OF OFFICE	SCHOOL NO. OR SOURCE	CASE NO.	NAME	SEX B.G.	AD-DRESS	HOURS			EMPLOY-MENT ADDRESS	COURT	DROPPED	LAWFUL	UNLAWFUL	DATE OF RET'N	DISPOSI-TION OF CASE
						AR-RIVED	LEFT	NAME							
TOTAL															

[Reverse of Form 36]

DAILY SUMMARY OF CLASSIFICATION OF CASES

SCHOOL NO. OR SOURCE	A—DROPPED FROM ROLL TO—									B—LAWFUL ABSENCE TO—								C—UNLAWFUL TO—					D—SPECIAL ACTION TO—							TO-TALS
	A1	A2	A3	A4	A5	A6	A7	A8	TAL	B1	B2	B3	B4	B5	B6	B7	TAL	C1	C2	C3	C4	TAL	D1	D2	D3	D4	D5	D6	TAL
TOTAL																													
CASE PENDING COMPLETED																													
CASE PENDING, GIVE SCHOOL NUMBER																													
TOTAL CASES CLOSED																													

NOTE.—The items indicated by the code letters and numbers may be printed over each one in order to avoid confusion and delay in referring to the code.

Form 36. Daily Report of Attendance Officer.—The amount and character of the work accomplished by the attendance officer is a real test of his efficiency. A statement of the time required for each case may be open to the objection that such cases cannot be fully verified, but the limited number of cases which each officer can investigate in a day renders it possible for him to make such a record without unjustifiable effort or trouble. Even if not strictly accurate the distribution of his time will show any tendency to devote too much time to the schools visited or to clerical and other duties when the time ought to be devoted to field work and a modification of procedure could follow. The daily report should show:

1. Name of the officer.
2. Names of schools visited.
3. Cases for each school reported, or other source.
    a. School number or central office number for each case.
    b. Case number for each absence.
    c. Definition of case.
4. Address of each case.
5. Number investigated for each school.
6. Disposition of case.
7. Time required and location of each case.
8. Classification of case.
9. Signature of officer.
10. Cases pending completed.
11. Cases pending incompleted.
12. Date and day of week of the report.
13. Cases.
14. Visits to homes.
15. Visits to schools.
16. Visits to places of employment.
17. Summary of classification.

Form 37. Monthly Report of Attendance Officer.—The monthly report of the attendance officer is a summary of the daily reports of the month, so arranged that the number of cases for each school are shown for each day of the month.

The reverse of Form 37 will be similar to the reverse of Form 36 except that the date will replace the school number or source and each day's totals will be distributed according to the daily summary of the classification of cases. Special recommendations of the attendance officer should form a part of each monthly report.

FORM 37. MONTHLY REPORT OF ATTENDANCE OFFICER

MONTHLY REPORT OF ATTENDANCE OFFICER. CITY OF_____																																
MONTH:									NAME																							
SOURCE OR SCHOOL	1	2	3	4	5	6	7	8	9	10	11	12	13	14	15	16	17	18	19	20	21	22	23	24	25	26	27	28	29	30	31	TOTAL
	TOTAL INVESTIGATIONS FOR MONTH																															
VISITS TO HOMES																																
SCHOOL																																
COURT																																
EMPLOYER																																
OTHER																																
TOTAL VISITS																																
CASES E-NUMERATED																																
CASES CHECKED																																

Form 38. Monthly Report of the Attendance Department to the Superintendent of Schools.—This report should be made at the end of the month, giving an accounting of the activities of the department. It should be a summary of all the officers' monthly reports and other necessary facts regarding the work of the department.

FORM 38. MONTHLY REPORT OF ATTENDANCE DEPART-
MENT TO SUPERINTENDENT OF SCHOOLS

CITY OF _____																																
MOMTHLY REPORT OF ATTENDANCE DEPARTMENT TO SUPERINTENDENT OF SCHOOLS																																
CASES OF ATTEND-									MONTH ENDING																							
ANCE OFF.	1	2	3	4	5	6	7	8	9	10	11	12	13	14	15	16	17	18	19	20	21	22	23	24	25	26	27	28	29	30	31	TOTAL

(The monthly summary of classification of cases similar to Form 36)

The following should be given with the above report:

1. Total number of boys and girls summoned for hearing.
2. Total number of parents summoned for hearing.
3. Total number of boys and girls placed on probation.
4. Total number of boys and girls committed to parental schools.
5. Total number of parental prosecutions.
6. Total number of boys' and girls' work certificates issued.
7. Total number of boys' and girls' work certificates renewed.
8. Total number of boys' and girls' work certificates revoked.

9. Total number of boys' and girls' work certificates denied.
10. Total number referred to social agencies.
11. Total number of legal notices served.

Form 39. Annual Report of Attendance Office to Superintendent of Schools.—A complete summary of all monthly reports will give all the necessary facts regarding the work of the attendance department for the year. With this should be a discussion of important phases of the work and recommendations for the improvement of the attendance service.

Form 40. Age-Grade-Absence Table.—One of the outstanding shortcomings of the administration of the schools of the cities studied was the lack of information available for the superintendent's study and analysis of the attendance status of his schools. It was not considered necessary to have an accurate and complete picture of the city-wide attendance conditions or of the condition of any particular school other than the percentage of attendance in its various forms. There was a noticeable lack of interest in the whole problem. A feeling expressed on the part of superintendents that attendance "was about as good as could be expected" gave the typical attitude of school administrators towards this aspect of their school problems. When a picture of all the lawful and unlawful absences by age, grade and total number of days' absence is disclosed, greater emphasis will, no doubt, be given towards determining the means whereby a better condition can be brought about.

In order that the superintendent may have at hand at the end of each term or year a basis of investigation of just what his attendance has been in terms of the number of days lost, both lawful and unlawful, and the incidence of such absence in terms of age and grade, the Age-Grade-Absence Table shown in Form 40 is recommended. This form is based upon the Strayer-Engelhardt Age-Grade Table and is so arranged that three groups of absentees are considered, the "occasional," the "frequent," and the "habitual." The number of days employed can be made subject to the local conception of what constitutes the absence allowance for these groups and may be adjusted to the length of the school year. In Form 40 a yearly absence of from 1 to 19 days is considered occasional; 20 to 49, frequent; and 50 or more, habitual.[15]

[15] Bureau of Compulsory Education, Philadelphia, 1923, p. 19.

ANNUAL AGE-GRADE-ABSENCE TABLE
FOR ELEMENTARY SCHOOLS

SCHOOL_____

COMPILED_____

KEY: ILLEGAL = I   LEGAL = L

DATE_____

GRADE SECTION	KINDERGARTEN 4 YRS 9 MOS. TO 5 YRS. 9 MOS.				KINDERGARTEN 5 YRS 3 MOS. TO 6 YRS. 3 MOS.				EIGHTH GRADE 13 YRS. 3 MOS. TO 14 YRS. 3 MOS.				TOTAL			
AGE	OCCASIONAL 1-19 DAYS	FREQUENT 20-49 DAYS	HABITUAL 50 DAYS AND OVER		OCCASIONAL 1-19 DAYS	FREQUENT 20-49 DAYS	HABITUAL 50 DAYS AND OVER		OCCASIONAL 1-19 DAYS	FREQUENT 20-49 DAYS	HABITUAL 50 DAYS AND OVER		OCCASIONAL 1-19 DAYS	FREQUENT 20-49 DAYS	HABITUAL 50 DAYS AND OVER	

FORM 40.   AGE-GRADE-ABSENCE TABLE

For the term half of these absences could be used. It may be arranged for half sessions if desired. The absences are also to be distributed in terms of lawful and unlawful absences. By distributing the number of pupils, grouped by age and grade, in accordance with the number of absences under the proper heading of legal and illegal, it is possible for the school authorities to see where there have been occasional, frequent, habitual, legal and illegal absences.

The legal absences are largely problems of health, and it is here that the Department of Health should have functioned and should have on record the service it has rendered to reduce the groups of absences due to ill health. The illegal absences are the responsibility of the attendance department.

For either group selected in any age or grade where there appeared an undue heaping up of cases the superintendent may ask for a special reporting giving full details of the individuals involved and the remedial measures offered. The form also shows the attendance status in terms of over-age, under-age, and normal age children, thereby offering a possible clew to an underlying cause for the conditions found.

Such a report will cause teachers to pay more careful attention to their responsibilities in accounting for all absences in terms of legal and illegal reasons, and to have available evidences of the efforts made to make such an accounting. In Form 24 each teacher will be able to make such a distribution for her class and the report of the school will be a summary of the classroom reports. A city distribution may be made from a summary of the tables of all schools.

Form 41. Monthly Grade-Report of Entries, Withdrawals and Attendance.—A detailed analysis of school membership constitutes a part of the superintendent's child-accounting balance sheet. Many forms are used for showing the actual registration with gains and losses in membership, with the location of the same, but the following information should be available, distributed by day of month and day of week.[16] The form with title, grade, name of teacher and date should be arranged under the following headings and sub-headings for each day of the month and day of the week with weekly and monthly totals:

[16] Moehlman, A. B., *Child Accounting,* Forms 10 and 12.

1. Registration:
   a. Boys.
   b. Girls.
2. Received by transfer from:
   a. Other rooms within same building.
   b. Local public schools.
   c. Local non-public schools.
   d. Public schools in this state.
   e. Non-public school in this state.
3. Returns.
4. Losses:
   a. Other rooms within the same building.
   b. Local public schools.
   c. Local non-public schools.
   d. Public schools in this state.
   e. Non-public schools in this state.
   f. Other states and countries.
   g. Reform school.
   h. Institution for defectives.
   i. Employment permits.
   j. Non-attendance permits.
   k. Marriage.
   l. Death.
   m. Under compulsory school age.
   n. Over compulsory school age.
   o. Others.
5. Daily membership.
6. Daily attendance:
   a. Number present, A.M.
   b. Number tardy.
   c. Number present, P.M.
   d. Number tardy.

The total of the last month and the total of each column for year to date give a cumulative record for the grade. The names of pupils received with source and pupils left with destination should be given on reverse side of form.

Forms 42 and 43. Monthly School and City Summary of Entries, Withdrawals and Attendance.—The monthly report will be the summary of all the grade reports of that school and when combined with other schools will constitute the summary for the city.

The information will be distributed by grades, kindergarten and Grades 1 to 6 with totals, Grades 7 to 9 with totals, and Grades 10 to 12 with totals; or by Grades 1 to 8 and 9 to 12 in accordance with the plan of school organization. Distribution should also be made for any special classes, continuation school, or junior college.

The blank should have the actual days of school attendance to date and all the items of the grade monthly, Form 41, report of entries, withdrawals and attendance, together with the following (For items 1-6, see Form 41):

> 7. Per cent of attendance for current month.
> 8. Membership at date of report.
> 9. Sum of daily membership since beginning of year.
> 10. Sum of daily attendance in days since beginning of year.

Form 44. Annual City Summary of Entries, Withdrawals, Attendance.—For the annual report the following additional spaces will be used:

> 11. Average membership for year.
> 12. Average attendance for year.
> 13. Average per cent of attendance for year.
> 14. Aggregate tardiness of pupils for year.

With such a form the records are cumulative and the exact status of each grade, each school and the city are known up to date. As the monthly and annual reports of the school attendance of the city are given by grade average rather than by schools, standards are not set up which are made objects of attainment sometimes by more or less questionable means.

DESIRABLE CUMULATIVE RECORDS

If, to the records given above, each school and the administrative office maintain records of the data obtained from year to year, the school principals and authorities will have at hand records that will render possible a more intelligent consideration of their particular problems. Among the data that will prove valuable in such cumulative records over a period of years are:

> 1. Total enrollment or registration: (*a*) by grades, (*b*) by month, (*c*) by years, (*d*) by school.
> 2. Total belonging or membership: (*a*) by grades, (*b*) by school, (*c*) by months, (*d*) by years.
> 3. Total number attending school: (*a*) by grade, (*b*) by month, (*c*) by year.

4. Monthly percentage of attendance for the entire school: (*a*) by grade, (*b*) by month, (*c*) by year.
5. Number of days school has been in session: (*a*) by months, (*b*) by school year.
6. Aggregate days' attendance: (*a*) by months, (*b*) by school year.
7. Distribution of attendance by ten-day groups: (*a*) by grades, (*b*) by months, (*c*) by school year.
8. Record of transfers: (*a*) local schools, (*b*) to or received from other school systems.
9. Distribution of permanent withdrawals: (*a*) by causes, (*b*) by grades, (*c*) by years.[17]

Such records constitute a continuous survey of the attendance status of a city. If each school maintains some or all of these records to that extent, the school authorities, on the occasions of special investigations, have recourse to comparative data covering a period of years that will prove of value.

[17] Forms for records 1-9, C. F. Williams Series, are found in the Strayer-Engelhardt Series. Teachers College, Columbia University.

CHAPTER V

ATTENDANCE SERVICE AND THE COURTS

Another purpose of the investigation was to learn the (*a*) relationship that existed between the courts and the attendance service in the group of cities selected, (*b*) the policies of enforcement that prevailed, (*c*) the problem of truancy and its treatment, (*d*) the results of probation, informal hearings and interviews, (*e*) and the forms and records found desirable to meet the best prevailing practices.

After reasonable effort has been made by the school authorities to bring the parent, the child and the employer to their responsibility, it is often necessary to appeal to the courts. We cannot here be concerned with the law or the court procedure to such an extent as we are with the failure of the court to enforce the law thus rendering futile the efforts of the attendance department. Effective enforcement of the law is impossible without the fair and impartial support of the court; but the court cannot be expected to take intelligent and impartial action without the facts.

There has been a tendency, as evidenced by court action in the cities studied, to regard compulsory education cases as of no particular importance in comparison with the "serious" cases with which the court calendars are now overcrowded. The experience in many cities seems to have been the same. Attendance officers reported in all cities that it is the tendency of the courts to take a sentimental view of the situation and to seek every possible excuse for the truant child, the neglectful parent, or the indifferent employer.

In City A a careful examination of the records of court action showed that the general practice was to impose a fine of fifteen dollars, but no records were found to show that this fine had been collected. Payment was usually suspended and after some weeks the fine was revoked, if attendance of the child had been satisfactory. Such a procedure had not established in the minds of

the parents a respect for the law. In some cases the children had
been absent from 12 to 128 days and had been reported by the
school principal from 8 to 14 times before they were brought to
court. This violation of the law was treated lightly, since the fines
were in most cases revoked.

In City C only one parent had been fined out of 100 parents
arrested between July, 1917, and December, 1923.

Without the active, purposeful coöperation of the courts,
"moral suasion" is the only recourse the attendance officer has
for securing regular attendance of those determined to avoid
school attendance. In all but two cities the attendance department
felt its impotence in securing such coöperation from the courts
that it could bring about satisfactory attendance on the part of
those who are determined, often with parental connivance, to
resist the enforcement of compulsory attendance.

In City B it was possible to examine the records of cases brought
before the courts during the time of the writer's investigations.
These indicated the extent of absence for one week's court cases
and the action taken.

Case	Days' Absence Reported	Court Action
1	26	Probation
2	28	"
3	26	"
4	12	"
5	24	"
6	35	"
7	21	"
8	40	"
9	32	"

A few cases may be examined in more detail. The records of
the attendance department were so incomplete that it was necessary
to ask the school for any records that were needed for the proper
presentation of the case in court, and yet the last report of the
teacher shows how troublesome the case must be before it is
brought into court.

Case 10.—"This boy entered my room Feb. 18th. His former teacher
reports that he attended only 4 days last term. That is why I am reporting
these three half days." Fifth Report: "This boy is on a transfer from
Chalkstone Avenue. He began his truancy immediately. We have not

seen him since and apparently your office has fared likewise. This is the last report I shall make for him for he is beyond anything we can do."
(Signed) .... Teacher

Case 7.—Age 14. Record for school attendance for eight years.
Half Day Absences for Each of Sixteen Terms:

29	104	39	8
58	38	30	38
24	36	26	45
32	24	9	21

Total: 537 half days

The boy was put on probation. Later he was sent to the parental school and was reported absent 10 days there.

Case 8.—Age 14.

1924	Report Number	Days Absent
Oct. 11..........	3	28
Oct. 15..........	4	31
Nov. 28..........	1	8
Dec. 1, 3........	3	3
Feb. 2-25........	1	30

NOTE.—"He has been seen on the street many times. March 1, 1924, placed on probation."

One has but to examine this last record to show how the irregularity of the teacher's methods in filling out the report blanks which were to be numbered consecutively for each child reported failed to give the attendance department an accurate record for presenting the case in court. When the department received the report of November 28 it was marked No. 1, and 8 days were given as the number of absences. The next report was numbered 3 and only 3 days reported as the cumulative record of non-attendance. Unless the officer had remembered the case because of the number of times it had been reported, the real importance of immediate and serious action would not be brought to his attention.

The above brief history of the court cases for one week is not exceptional but typical of the court cases investigated in this city. From them it is evident that the attendance department is unable to cope with its problems and that the court lends but little real assistance by its "probation" decisions. To be brought into court seems to be merely an annoyance with very little if any value to prevent, or noticeably decrease, the amount of truancy or non-attendance. When the case became unbearable the child would be sent to the reform school, but such cases were very limited in number. Before such drastic measures were taken the boy was sent to the local "discipline" schools, where his record for truancy was little, if any, better than in the regular school.

POLICIES OF ENFORCEMENT

Two policies prevail in school attendance enforcement. On the one hand, the persuasive and corrective measure, with harsher methods as a last resort, are considered desirable. The attendance officer calls the attention of parents of non-attendants to the meaning and purpose of the law and strives to bring them to a realization of the necessity of fully coöperating with the school authorities in securing full compliance with the law.

On the other hand, there are the proponents of a strict and literal interpretation of the law. These demand prompt and drastic treatment of parent and child in the belief that in this way a more wholesome respect for the law will be created.

In all the cities but one there was a decided tendency to follow the more modern viewpoint—that attendance might be secured by force; but if the school fails to arouse a real vital interest in the school life, the benefits to the child from enforced attendance may well be questioned. Such a tendency was best illustrated by City K. In 1914, 268 cases were referred to the Juvenile Court. In 1919, under a change of policy, 103 cases were brought before the court and in 1924, 25 cases were referred to the court.

Although these two opposing policies prevail, all agreed that court action must be resorted to when repeated and willful violation of the law was the result of selfishness and parental greed.

TRUANCY

The causes of truancy have been the object of many careful studies. To-day we are able to analyze the problem as never before. It may be due to the inability of the child to adjust himself to the school conditions in which he finds himself.[1] It may be the economic urge, or a broken home, or a vicious neighborhood environment, or perhaps an inherited mental weakness. No

[1] Irwin, Elizabeth A., *Truancy*.

matter what the cause may be, it is now a recognized fact that the school can aid in solving the truancy problem by a better adaptation of its educational offerings to the needs of the normal and sub-normal child. In not more than two cities had any real attempt been made to solve its truancy problem in this way. When the case became sufficiently chronic recourse was made to the courts.

In Cities A, E, I, and K the attendance department made provisions for those truant children whose future regularity is open to doubt. Herein lay one of the outstanding opportunities for "case study." Written records of the efforts made were not available. In the above cities the chief attendance officer or a specially assigned officer had charge of the work. Their efforts, they claimed, had kept down the number of commitments and had secured a higher percentage of attendance. Lack of complete case records was noticeable in all the cities except City K, where special case reports for all special investigations made were on file. The lack of clearly supported facts had been no doubt a cause of many failures to secure court action when the case could no longer be handled by the attendance department.

City K had assigned one officer for half time as court attendance officer. In the other cities it was the practice to allow each officer to present his own truancy cases in court. In City K no case was referred to the Juvenile Court until the attendance department had exhausted all its resources in the handling of the case. When it became necessary to refer a case to the Juvenile Court, it was considered that the problem involved was of sufficient importance for the judge's immediate attention.

The practice of permitting cases which come up before the Juvenile Court for the first time, to be turned over to a probation officer as a penalty, was held in little repute by the attendance departments in all the cities studied. The results were unsatisfactory and not conducive to the best result, because of a lack of understanding on the part of the probation officer of the underlying causes and remedy for truancy and juvenile delinquency.

By the appointment of one of the attendance officers as special court attendance officer, with the authority of a volunteer probation officer, cases that under ordinary procedure would be referred to the Juvenile Court were handled by him. As a result in this city only twenty-eight cases were referred to the courts by the attendance officers. In the previous year one hundred cases had been referred to the courts.[2]

And yet with this spirit of relieving the court of a great part of its duty in connection with truancy, the officer continued his report: "It will take some time for the courts to appreciate our point of view on attendance cases and until they do we can hope for little relief from that quarter." There are some parents who consider the interest which the state assumes in the education of their children as "a rank and most presumptive abuse" of authority. The efforts of the teacher or attendance officer to bring about regular attendance are met with contempt and defiance. If the law is to be of any avail, it must cover cases of this type. The attendance officer reports that his efforts with the courts have been without satisfactory results.

PROBATION

In Cities B, L, and D the placing of a child on probation was so perfunctory that little or no benefit could be claimed. In City B, 3,882 cases of truancy were acted upon in one year. There were 301 prosecutions of 215 persons for violations of the compulsory attendance laws. Of this number 136 were new cases, 39 were cases previously excused, and 35 were cases continued on probation from the previous year. Of the 136 new cases 102 were placed on probation and excused later. One was committed to a reform school. What probation means in this city may be inferred from the fact that of the thirty-nine cases previously excused and arrested again this year, twenty-nine were once more placed on probation, eight were placed on probation and excused later, and three were committed to a reform school. Eight thousand and seven legal notices were sent to parents and five arrests were made in 1922–23. The one officer claims his ability to satisfactorily handle the attendance service.

Whatever may have been the benefits derived from the probationary period required by court action, it is impossible to determine the value in results accomplished towards the cure or prevention of truancy. In only one city was the department able to

[2] Attendance Department, City K, typewritten report, 1923.

answer questions regarding the physical and economic conditions,[3] the scholarship, age and grade of truants. Cities B and D had made a distribution by age of the 302 cases it claimed as truants.

City L had been satisfied to allow the attendance officer to make a report as follows for the year 1923–24 with no other records available.

REPORT OF ATTENDANCE OFFICER
CITY L—1923–24

Number of arrests 59
Arraigned in court 59
Found guilty 43
Placed on probation 28
Discharged 1
Committed to home 3
Suspended sentence 6

In the record of one officer, twenty-six had been found guilty but only six were placed on probation and one committed to a home. There was no accounting for the action taken in the cases of the others who were found guilty. The number of reported truants for the year was 811.

In City F the report contained only the statement that thirty-eight legal notices had been served and that there had been fourteen court cases. Somewhere in a small memorandum the attendance officer could usually find the names, addresses, and dates of those who had been brought into court. The only apparent object of such a record was to enable the attendance officer to make the type of annual reports as given above.

INFORMAL HEARINGS AND INTERVIEWS

Cities A, E, I, and K had succeeded in reducing the number of court cases by a system of informal hearings and interviews with parents against whom complaints had been brought for not complying with the attendance laws. These interviews are conducted by the chief attendance officer at the school or in his own office. Before court action is brought the attendance officer gives the parents an opportunity to be heard by notifying them to appear for such a hearing. These hearings may be held in the evenings or on Saturdays. Cases which are exceptionally diffi-

[3] Snedden and Allen, *School Reports and School Efficiency*, p. 124.

cult for the attendance officers and which would make too heavy
a demand upon their time are considered at these interviews. The
complete records for the case are accessible and the parents are
often willing to furnish information which they refuse to give
to the officer at the time of his visit to the home.

Not only have these hearings been effectual in keeping many
cases out of court but they have made it possible for the attendance department, through its coöperation with other social agencies, to render timely and helpful service to parents and children
in need.

SUMMARY AND RECOMMENDATIONS

No other phase of the work of the attendance department was
so lacking in records or so indefinite in its policy as the relation
of the department to the legal enforcement of the compulsory
education laws. In City C the attendance officer took a group
of boys before the court every week for a "talking to," and in
City M the chief of police was used in a similar way. From
this extreme we go to the other—City K, where every truant
with a record of non-attendance is given to a "special worker"
whose duty it is to make a careful study of all conditions, physical, mental and environmental, that may reveal the underlying
causes responsible for the failure of the child to attend school.
The child is brought into court only when all other methods fail.

Regardless of the policy of enforcement that may prevail, the
attendance department is not in a position to take intelligent
action until it has adequate information regarding all the conditions that underlie the problem in hand. It should also maintain
a record of its procedures in order to have an accounting of the
work done. For such a program the following forms and records
should be available:

45. Special Case Report.
46. Notice or Warning to Parents.
47. Hearing Summons.
48. Record of Informal Hearings.
49. Record of Prosecutions.
50. Daily Record of Pupils on Probation.
51. Truant and Court Record Card.
52. Record of Child Committed to Truant School or Institu-
    tion.

The legal forms required by the state laws for court action against the child or the parent need not be described here. They must of course conform to local requirements.

Form 45. Special Case Report.—Such a record should have detailed information concerning the individuality of the child and the efforts made to secure regular attendance and to influence his home conditions. A report of the child's home environment is particularly valuable in a determination of what action should be taken. A report to show the school history of the child or a copy of the Pupil's Report Card enables the attendance department to determine the retardation and the desirability of making new school adjustments. Inquiry often develops information of an unsatisfactory relation between teacher and child which has caused a permanent antagonism with its consequent maladjustments.[4]

It is customary in nearly all the cities to physically examine truants before sending them away to a truant or parental school. They should have every physical handicap removed before they are regarded as cases for punitive treatment. Both a physical and mental examination should be given before declaring a child a truant. A complete Special Case Report, page 120, should contain the information desired.

Form 46. Notice or Warning to Parents.—When an attendance officer fails to find a parent or guardian at home and is unable upon a second visit to get in touch with a parent, a legal notice is sent. Such a form is also used for those employed illegally or not attending school. These forms are often furnished by the state, and should give:

1. City, date, title.
2. Name of parent or guardian or person having control.
3. Address of parent or guardian or person having control.
4. Notification statement.
5. Name of child.
6. Name of school.
7. Provisions of the compulsory education law.
8. Signature of the Attendance Officer.

Under the laws of some states a notice in writing must be sent to the parent for three days' absence, or the equivalent, without

[4] First Annual Report, Department of Education, New York City, p. 194.

FORM 45. SPECIAL CASE REPORT

```
 1. Name and Address of the Child................................
 2. Date of Birth........................................
 3. School and Grade ....................................
 4. Character of Child:
     a. Normal ........................................
     b. Troublesome ...................................
     c. Incorrigible ..................................
     d. Vicious Habits ................................
 5. Truancy Record ......................................
    Cause of Absence:
     a. Truant ........................................
     b. Parental Indifference .........................
     c. Neglect .......................................
     d. Illegal Employment ............................
     e. Illness .......................................
 6. Court Record ........................................
 7. School Aptitudes.....................................
 8. Dissatisfied with School (Reasons)..................
 9. Failing of Promotion (Grades).......................
10. Health:.......... Physical............ Mental.............
11. Member of....... Boy Scouts ...........Club ........Church
12. Employed ..........................................
13. Father:..............Nationality ...............Language
14. Mother:..............Nationality ...............Language
15. Brothers and Sisters:.........Ages..............School Records
16. Home Conditions:
     a. Father:...........deceased ..............living elsewhere
        ..........employed ........intemperate ........invalid
     b. Mother:...........deceased ..............living elsewhere
        ..........employed ........intemperate ........invalid
```

[*Reverse of Card*]

The reverse should give details of action taken by the attendance service, including physical and psychological examinations.

legal excuse. If the child fails to appear at school within three days from the time the notice is served, unless legal excuse is presented, a warrant must be served and the parent or guardian must appear before a magistrate's court. Evidence of violation of the compulsory attendance law results in a sentence to pay a fine not to exceed two dollars. In case of the unlawful absence of a single session thereafter, prosecution may be instituted without a second written notice.[5]

Form 47. Hearing Summons.—When the attendance department desires the presence of a parent at a hearing to be held at a

[5] Digest of Laws Controlling School Attendance, Pennsylvania, 1922, p. 15.

school or at the attendance office, a form similar to that given below can be used.

FORM 47.   HEARING SUMMONS[6]

City of...................   Date.....................   No.......
To..........................   and...............................

Greetings: Pursuant to authority vested in me by the Education Law, you and each of you are hereby summoned to appear at the office of the Attendance Department, located at..............................
on the day, evening, of...............192....at.............to answer a complaint against you by Attendance Officer........................ for violation of the Education Law.
(Failure to respect this summons will result in complaint being made against the parent or guardian in.............................Court)

Signed.......................................

[6] See New York City, Bureau of Education, Form 309.

When printed with a stub giving number, attendance officer, names of persons summoned, address, date of hearing, date of service and person upon whom served, a complete record of case is at hand.   If made in duplicate and filed, the same object will be served.

Form 48.   Record of Informal Hearings.   In order that there may be a complete record of these informal hearings, a calendar may be kept.   This blank should give the following:

1. Date of each hearing.
2. Name of child, parent or guardian.
3. Address of child.
4. Number and description of the case.
5. The complaint.
6. Disposition of case.—Name of Attendance Officer.
7. Name of officer conducting hearings.

For the larger cities a form for each hearing may be used, but in the smaller cities a book ruled for the above record will adequately serve the purpose.

Form 49.   Record of Prosecutions.—Similarly a complete record of all court prosecutions should be maintained, giving:

1. The court numbers of new and adjourned cases:
   a. New.   *b.* Adjourned.
2. The name of parent or guardian of the child brought before the court.

3. The name of the child.
4. The address of the child, street and number.
5. The disposition of the case.
6. Name of attendance officer under whose supervision the case was brought.[7]

Form 50.   Daily Record of Pupils on Probation.—For the information of the attendance officer in charge of probation cases a daily record of pupils on parole or probation is desirable.   It may take the following form:

FORM 50.   DAILY RECORD OF PUPILS ON PROBATION

Daily Record of Pupil on Probation. City of.............						
Name	Last First		School	Grade · Dateparoled		
Address				Attendance district		
Date	Attendance		Conduct	Effort	Signatures	
	A.M.	P.M.			Teacher	Parent

This card should be filed under date when next report is due. A new card is issued each time the pupil reports until case is closed.

Form 51.   Truant and Court Record Card.—In order that a record may be kept of all truant and other cases brought before the courts a card giving the following information will suffice:

FORM 51.   TRUANT AND COURT RECORD CARD

Truant and Court Record Card.   City of
Name........................Date................School......
Parent or Guardian........................•
Address..............St.........No.......Age......Grade.....
Complaint........................,
Court.................Disposition........................
Remarks........................

By referring to the "Special Case" record all the information leading up to court action may be obtained.   The results of probation or commitment to a truant school will be available from Forms 50 and 52.

[7] Strayer and Engelhardt, *School Records and Reports*, pp. 33-35.   Also Forms and Records: New York City Attendance Department.

Form 52. Record of a Child Committed to Truant School or Institution.—After the attendance department has found it necessary to secure the commitment of a child to an institution for truancy or juvenile delinquency, it should be able to show some records of the results of such action when the time of commitment expires. Such a record card filed alphabetically in a "current file" and later in a file of "expired cases" should contain the following information:

1. Title of card.
2. First and last name of child.
3. Date of birth in month, day and year.
4. The school and grade attended.
5. Name of parent or guardian.
6. Date of commitment.
7. Name of magistrate committing child.
8. Date commitment was executed.
9. Name of school or institution to which child was committed.
10. Date of parole.
11. Date of any re-commitment.
12. Final date of parole or discharge.
13. A complete record of date and grade of conduct and work during the time the child is in the control of the institution.

In large cities where there are a number of truancy cases, it may be found desirable to have special forms for (*a*) physical and mental examination of truants, (*b*) report on home environments of the child. If these forms are made in triplicate on carbonized paper, the report is made available for the investigator, the school, and the attendance department without transcription.

When the above records are maintained the attitude of the attendance service will of necessity change. Each officer may not at once adapt himself to this new conception of attendance service, but he will gradually see in the critical inquiry of the causes underlying truancy and juvenile delinquency, an opportunity to render greater service to the child and a higher service to the community.

CHAPTER VI

ATTENDANCE SERVICE AND CHILD EMPLOYMENT

The last problem of our investigation in the fifteen cities selected for study was to determine the following:

1. The present status of the practices of the attendance service in regard to:
   (a) The method of issuing employment certificates.
   (b) The census and illegal employment.
   (c) Illegal employment and non-public schools.
   (d) The proof of age required for employment certificates.
   (e) Child health and the issuing of employment certificates.
   (f) The termination of employment and return of certificate.
   (g) The educational requirement for employment certificate.
2. The attendance service and part-time education.
3. The forms and reports considered necessary to insure efficient attendance service under the requirement of the child labor laws.

Early in our educational history there was constant agitation for legislation to restrain children from severe labor and to make satisfactory provision for their continued contact with the schools. Many agencies have delayed progress. Exceptions from the requirement of the compulsory school law are numerous. The most persistent, other than the exemption for mental and physical inability, is the permission of the child between certain compulsory school years to secure employment. Because child labor and compulsory school attendance are two aspects of our compulsory education problem, the laws governing the two have been worked out so as to secure a fair degree of harmony of administration; but in actual practice this is too often lacking.

It is one of the conclusions from studies in child labor, that were states to embody in their requirements for working papers the highest standards thus far attained in actual practice, children would be required to meet the following conditions before leaving school:

1. "Certificate to be issued by some centralized authority, either by state officials or under close state supervision, to all children between 14 and 17 who leave school to engage in work of any kind."

2. "Issue of such certificates only to those who have completed the elementary school course, unless at least 15 years of age."

3. "Adequate documentary proof of age."

4. "A definite written promise of suitable. employment."

5. "A medical examination showing the child to be fit to undertake the work proposed."

6. "Certificate to be sent by office of issue to the employer by mail and to be returned to the office of issue in the same manner on termination of employment."

7. "The child to remain in school until the papers are issued." [1]

Unfortunately the child labor problem is weighed in many states by different standards. Some of the outstanding features of the present status are brought to light by recent legislators.

"There is no doubt that the number of child workers in this country now far exceeds the millions [2] named by the census of 1920. This census was taken not only while the Second Federal Child Labor Law was in effect but also at the beginning of a period of general industrial depression when thousands of children were temporarily released from work. These census figures include also only child laborers from 10 to 15 years of age. Those under 10 years working at such occupations as agriculture, domestic service, street trading and factory work done at home, are unrecorded. This would probably augment by thousands the million children of the 1920 census." [3]

With the striking inequalities in the length of school terms, as shown in Chapter I, and the extent of child labor in many states, it is well to examine the legislative measures enacted during

[1] Ensign, F. C., *School Attendance and Child Labor*, p. 241.
[2] *Research Bulletin of the N. E. A.,* Vol. I, No. 4, p. 287.
[3] Table 13, Federal Census, 1920.

the last year to bring out the weak spots in our status and bring nearer an "equality of educational opportunity" for the boys and girls of every state. By many of these provisions the state is emphasizing its control and raising the minima that are guaranteed every child.

RECENT CHILD LABOR LEGISLATION

A brief survey of the state child labor legislation of 1924 shows the usual backward and forward movements of social and educational progress. Since the federal child labor law was declared unconstitutional, there seems to have been a slowing up in child labor legislative activity. Some have endeavored to explain the lessening activity by the greater difficulty of persuading legislatures to act, now that a state of high standards is compelled to compete with those of much lower standards without danger of federal interference. Compulsory attendance enforcement parallels all child labor legislation. Although the child labor laws cannot keep children in school, they can, with a fair rate of effectiveness, prohibit the children from going to work. Only six of the forty-eight states took any definite action for the further protection of child labor.

The principal features of legislation enacted during the last year are as follows:

Mississippi.—A 14-year age limit in factories, canneries, etc., extended to include boys as well as girls. An 8-hour day, 44-hour week and prohibition of night work under 16 years.

New Jersey.—A law providing double compensation for injured minors illegally employed.

New York.—Regulation of hours for minors under 18 in factories extended to mercantile establishments and transportation or distribution of merchandise. Night work prohibition amended to forbid employment between midnight and six A.M. (instead of 4 A.M.) Complete enforcement of the continuation law deferred for 3 years.

North Carolina.—Abolition of the provision allowing State Welfare Commission to make exemptions in age standards for employment. Employers must secure employment certificates for all under 16. Physical examination required for all under 16 and prohibition from work under hazardous conditions.

Rhode Island.—Bill providing for 9-hour day and 48-hour week for those under 16.

Alabama.—Physical examination by public school or county health officer or duly licensed physician. Examination must conform to standards prescribed by State Board of Health and extension of summer permits to dairies and golf caddying. Educational requirements for work certificates raised from 4th to 5th grade, September, 1924, and to 6th grade, September, 1926.

Not alone do we get a deeper insight into our compulsory education problem through a survey of the legislative measures passed, but we get further enlightenment as to the conditions yet to be improved by the measures that are lost. Among those that failed to receive legislative acceptances are:

Kentucky.—Street trade law to provide 14-year limit for boys, 18-year limit for girls in cities of 1st, 2nd and 3rd class.

Louisiana.—The completion of 5th grade or equivalent required for work permits. Reduction of maximum work hours from 60 to 54. Mother pension bill.

Maryland.—Bill to raise the school requirement from the fifth to the sixth grade.

Massachusetts.—Bill to repeal the 48-hour law allowing women and children to work between 6 and 11 at night. Bill to raise the school requirement first to 14, then to 15 and 16 years.

New Jersey.—Bill to forbid children under 16 in public performances. Seventh grade requirements for work certificates. A bill to increase fine for violation of sweat shop laws. A biennial census law.

New York.—Bill to forbid night work under 18. Bill to apply compensation law to any employment where two or more are at work.

Rhode Island.—Bill to allow physically fit children over 14, mentally incapable of learning to read and write, or of making further progress in school, to go to work.

Virginia.—Bill to forbid children under 14 from working in any gainful occupations other than farms, orchards, gardens [4] or delivery of dairy, poultry or garden products.

ENFORCEMENT OF CHILD EMPLOYMENT LAWS

As soon as state legislatures began to enact compulsory attendance laws enforcement was left to the local authorities. To them also was entrusted the responsibility of the child labor laws. Gradually there developed a central state office for the supervision

[4] National Child Labor Committee, *The American Child*, Vol. VII, January, 1925, p. 6.

of child labor, leaving, for the most part, however, the administration of school attendance to local control.

Since 1866, when Massachusetts inaugurated state enforcement, the other states have [5] gradually fixed age requirements, prescribed the minimum educational requirements and the officer to whom should be entrusted the labor permits.[6]

PRESENT STATUS IN FIFTEEN CITIES

In 1915 the United States Children's Bureau began a comprehensive and systematic study of the administration of the child labor laws. The results of that study should be the establishment of standards for the administration of laws with special reference to the system of employment certificates. Even then the attainment of these standards will depend upon their acceptance and the conscientious and efficient administration of the law.[7]

The three outstanding requisites for employment certificates are at the present time (a) attainment of a minimum age, (b) attainment of a minimum education, and (c) physical fitness for the work at which the child is to be employed and general satisfactory health. The officer or clerk by virtue of the work of issuing certificates actually becomes the local administrator of the child labor law. In all the fifteen cities, with the exception of City K, the issuing of certificates was the responsibility of the attendance office. In Cities A, B, E, L, and O, this work was handled by a clerk under the supervision of the attendance officer whose other duties left him little time to make more than a perfunctory examination of the work done. In the other cities children with or without parents were found securing employment papers with the only insistence that the papers should be complete and that the records filed should disclose no irregularities when the state authorities made an investigation. There was a wholesome respect for the state's investigation of the administration of the employment certification. The fact that the factory inspector was often seeking information regarding certain employed minors,—as happened in City E and City M during the writer's

[5] Ensign, F. C., *Compulsory School Attendance and Child Labor*, p. 57,
[6] For distribution of these requirements by states, see Bulletin 2, Bureau of Education, pp. 80 to 86.
[7] Consult Children's Bureau Publications, Connecticut No. 12, New York No. 17, Maryland No. 41, and Wisconsin No. 85.

visits,—had an apparent effect upon the attitude of attendance department towards increasing the care with which violation of the law was avoided.

From the evidence obtained in the study of these cities one would be compelled to agree with the statement that: "All available evidence indicates that, defective as the enforcement of the child labor laws often is, vastly better results are obtained in this field by state agents than in the enforcement of attendance by local authorities." [8]

In Cities I, J, L, M, N, and O, where state agents were supposed to investigate the attendance service, there was no evidence that the state exercised the same control over attendance that it did over child labor. There was laxity of enforcement in both, but the attitude toward the labor permits and the investigations of the illegally employed was (in all the cities visited) taken more seriously than truancy or irregular attendance. The efforts to safeguard the labor laws appeared to take precedence over any other phase of the attendance service.

Issuing Employment Certificates.—The procedure for obtaining employment certificates did not vary in principle in the different cities. An application is filled out, followed or preceded by a promise of employment and then a school record, proof of age, and a certificate of physical fitness. After these had been obtained the employment certificate was issued.

Cities differed in their attitudes towards the application for an employment certificate. In Cities E, J, and O no application was accepted unless the child was accompanied by its parent. An investigation of the family status was made and the application denied if any excuse to keep the child in school was available. In City O 124 certificates were refused in one year. The understaffed attendance department in City D was unable to take full charge of the issuing of work certificates. For this reason the attendance office furnished the schools with a supply of all employment papers. Upon certain days the school physician went to the school and at a given signal those desiring working certificates went to the office for examination. All the papers were given to the child and a duplicate of the application blank sent to the attendance office by the attendance officer. This duplicate form

[8] Ensign, F. C., *School Attendance and Child Labor*, p. 243.

was devised to inform the attendance office that papers had been issued and—to make them legal—required the signature of the chief attendance officer. This system failed because the child was often given both forms, or one was given to the child and one was retained by the school instead of being sent to the attendance office.

Cases where the child took the papers and secured employment without the signature of the proper official were being reported frequently. Six of these cases were under investigation at the time of the writer's visit. No record to show the number that entered employment without the signature of the attendance officer was available.

The Census and Illegal Employment.—The lack of accurate continuing census information in all the cities made it impossible to determine the number of illegally employed. In all the cities the attendance department was finding children so employed and no record was maintained to show how long such children had been thus employed. To report the number brought under the operation of the law was considered sufficient.

Illegal Employment and Non-Public Schools.—Complaint was constantly heard that children fourteen years of age enrolled in non-public schools were going to work without employment certificates when crowded school conditions or the economic status of a family seemed to justify a child's leaving school. Lack of full coöperation of all the schools in the city and lack of information regarding the number of children of all ages, with the checking for those not in school, made possible a constant source of illegal employment. There appeared to be an earnest endeavor on the part of the school authorities to live up to the law in so far as their knowledge regarding the actual children employed permitted.

Proof of Age.—In all cities it was claimed that documentary proof of age was demanded. Only as a last resort was the affidavit of a parent or guardian or a physician's certificate of age, accepted. In City B where a record for a year was available we find that the following "proofs of age" had been accepted:

1. Birth certificates 1,721
2. Baptismal certificates 321
3. Passports 21
4. Secretary of State Board of Education......... 20

The age certificate required by the laws of Pennsylvania, page 176, was one of the most helpful legal provisions to overcome the complaint, so often heard, that employers employed children under sixteen years of age upon the claim of the child that he was over sixteen and entitled to go to work. Such certificates prevent dishonest foremen from employing minors illegally and also prevent parents from obtaining work for minor children by making false statements regarding the children's ages.

Child Health and Employment.—Under the best administration of the laws the applicant for employment certificate must submit to a thorough physical examination and be certified as to his physical fitness for the work to be undertaken. The letter of the law is generally followed. Certificates are required, but the physical examination is too perfunctory to meet the full spirit of the law.

The report of City A shows conditions that are recognized as existent in the other cities. "The physical examination of children applying for employment certificates continues to be unsatisfactory. The law provides that before an employment certificate can be issued the child must present a certificate from a school physician showing that the child has undergone a thorough physical examination. The present method is to send these children to the offices of the school physicians, dividing the number as equally as possible between the different physicians. Children spend considerable time in getting to the physicians' offices. They may have to wait for the physician to come in or wait until he has seen patients who may have been waiting for him. Then the physician is usually busy and gives the child the most superficial examination. The physicians dislike to be bothered at their offices, children are delayed in getting their employment certificates and do not receive the protection which the law was intended to give them." [9]

A Certificate of Physical Fitness, based upon the standards of physical fitness established by the Pennsylvania Department of Labor and Industry and prescribed for the guidance of local issuing officers, will give the legal safeguard [10] which the most progressive states consider desirable.

[9] Typewritten Report of Attendance Department, City A.
[10] Pennsylvania, Department of Labor and Industry, Article III, Standards of Physical Fitness. 1925.

It was unusual for a child in any city to be refused employment certificate because of physical conditions.

The Termination of Employment and Return of Certificate.— In every case the attendance departments expressed their belief that there were many out of employment for whom the employer had failed to return the notice of termination of employment or to return the working permits.[11]   There is no evidence to show that penalties for non-compliance with the law are enforced.

In City B, where school attendance service took little thought of regularity of attendance, a complaint against employers was based on the grounds that "many children lost positions because their former employers do not return their employment certificates to the issuing officer within the time required by law."

In City C the question of renewal of employment certificates was left to the continuation school and the attendance office had no knowledge of what was done.

In City K the law required the return of the certificate within two weeks of termination of employment to have the certificate renewed.   If the child does not find another job within two weeks he is returned to day school.

In City O the attendance department refuses to renew an employment certificate unless the child has a good attendance record at the continuation school.   Two other practices were found in this city which were indicative of the general attitude towards the issuance of employment certificates.   They were only issued on Saturday mornings so that no school time was lost.   If a child had been absent from school looking for work, papers would not be issued for two weeks, during which time an investigation would be made to ascertain the family conditions.

Under the same state law the attendance department of City N does not know how long pupils are out of school before getting papers.   A daily list of applications is the only check on those leaving school to go to work, the attendance department getting few if any reports from the schools of those leaving for this purpose.

The cities visited had no uniform practice in the recording of certificates granted.   "Re-issues" (subsequent) and original certificates in Cities F, G, O, and D were reported together.   City N

[11] Massachusetts General Law, Chaps. 76 and 149.

showed that there were 1,047 "re-issues" and 1,212 original certificates. Such an analysis of the record should be made to show both the subsequent and original certificates. A large total of certificates issued does not of necessity mean a large increase in the number of children at work. During periods of unemployment there is less tendency and opportunity for the child to change his job. A large number of re-issues indicates possibilities for children to be out of work and out of school. Such periods of idleness create serious social problems and it becomes the duty of the attendance department to adjust its activities to this new responsibility. Coöperation of its own placement service or coördination activities with the other social agencies of the city can do much to make suitable adjustments to meet the individual difficulties with a lessening of the often expensive turnover of the employer.

Minimum Educational Requirements.—The legal requirements show varying educational standards. The early provision was that the child applying for employment certificate must give evidence that he had attended school a minimum of months, usually three months of the preceding year. From this the compulsory laws steadily advance these until we have, as in New York, the requirement of the elementary school course of eight grades or the equivalent.[12]

The legal requirements were met officially, at least, in all the cities, although complaint was heard that troublesome children below the grade required to meet the legal requirements were given age and schooling certificates.

In City B the minimum educational requirement—the completion of the sixth grade—was considered too high and eighteen permits were issued to so-called backward children who could neither read at sight nor write simple sentences. This was based on the ground that "much suffering had been caused poor families by compelling the eldest children in the homes to remain in school after they had reached their fourteenth birthday." No evidence was at hand to show that any special adjustment of the school program has been made for these children to enable them to meet the demands of future employment with some degree of economic security.

[12] Ensign, F. C., *School Attendance and Child Labor*, p. 240.

It will be necessary to make provision for exceptional cases, but the requirement of an eighth grade education is not too high in a country where universal suffrage plays so important a part.

ATTENDANCE SERVICE AND PART-TIME EDUCATION

No other phase of education has brought a more difficult problem to the attendance service of some of our cities than the compulsory part-time school. In 1911 Wisconsin passed the first part-time education laws in the United States. It was followed by Pennsylvania in 1915. At the present time twenty-three states are shown in Table XX as requiring continuation education.

TABLE XX
COMPULSORY ATTENDANCE PROVISION IN CONTINUATION SCHOOLS [14]

States	Law in Effect	Minimum Number of Minors Required to Establish Classes	Age of Required Attendance	Hours of Required Attendance a Week	Length of School Year
Arizona	1919	15	14–16	5	150 hours
California	1920	12 [1]	14–18	4	Same as public school
Delaware	1921	15	12–16	4	36 weeks
Florida	1921	15 [2]	14–16	..	144 hours
Illinois	1921	20	14–18	8	Same as public school
Iowa	1919	15	14–16	8	" " " "
Massachusetts	1920	200 [3]	14–16	4	" " " "
Michigan	1920	50	14–18	8	" " " "
Missouri	1919	25	14–16	4	" " " "
Montana	1919	15	14–18	4	" " " "
Nebraska	1919	15	14–16	8	144 hours
Nevada	1919	15	14–18	4	Same as public school
New Jersey	1920	20	14–16	6	36 weeks
New Mexico	1919	15	14–16	5	150 hours
New York	1920	200 [4]	14–18	4–8	Same as public school
Ohio	1921	[5]	16–18	4	144 hours
Oklahoma	1919	20	16–18	..	" "
Oregon	1919	15 [2]	14–18	5	Same as public school
Pennsylvania	1915	30	14–16	8	" " " "
Utah	1919	15	14–18	4	144 hours
Washington	1920	15 [6]	14–18	4	Same as public school
West Virginia	1921	50	14–16	4–8	144 hours
Wisconsin	1911	[4]	14–18	[7]	8 months

[1] High school districts having fifty or more pupils must establish part-time classes.
[2] Attendance upon evening school may be substituted.
[3] Referendum law adopted by all towns affected except one.
[4] Establishment required only in cities of 5,000 population.
[5] Permissive, Mandatory.
[6] Districts may organize schools upon written request of 25 students.
[7] 14- and 15-year-old children part-time; 16- and 17-year-old children 8 hours a week. (12.)

[14] Keller, F. J., *Day Schools for Young Workers*, p. 7 and Bureau of Education, Bulletin No. 5, 1921, Appendix B.

Essentially, the problem of attendance in these schools is similar to that of the full-time schools. The positive factors of effective instruction, good discipline, and school spirit will contribute most to school attendance. To these pupils "time is money." The continuation school was established without the complete coöperation of employers, and there is no reason to believe that employers will not, for some time, discriminate in favor of those who can devote full time to their services.

In the cities studied there was evidence that these schools were endeavoring to make practical adjustments of the time of attending to the requirements of the employer or parent. There was no rigid insistence upon a program that would be out of keeping with the wishes of the employer. This in itself avoided resentment and tendencies to poor attendance.

Not as yet, however, has the continuation school, where these schools are established, been fully recognized as a vital part of the school system. Little effort has been made to acquaint the pupils of all our schools with the methods, ideals and advantages of the continuation school, as has been done for the high school and higher institutions. When this becomes more generally a part of good school administration many of the antagonisms and misconceptions now held by prospective continuation school pupils will be corrected. The initial difficulties of attendance will be lessened and the transfer from one school to the other will be more easily made.

Making up Attendance.—All continuation schools required "make up" for illegal absence. City O required it for legal as well as illegal absence. It was the consensus of opinion that a rule requiring that all absences be made up is one of the most potent factors in decreasing non-attendance. The amount of absence is recorded and the pupil is required in some cases to make up at least one hour regardless of the amount of absence or tardiness though it [15] be only ten or fifteen minutes. Others have found it satisfactory to limit the make up to exactly the amount of time missed. The idea must be to offer pupils some work to take the place of the instruction lost and not merely to prevent further absence by compelling the pupil to return to school at inconvenience to himself and employer. The work must actually

[15] Part-Time Schools, Bulletin No. 73, Federal Board of Vocational Education, p. 248.

be worth while or the possible arousing of the deep antagonism of pupil and employer may be more harmful than the hours lost.

Methods of Securing Attendance.—In the reports of twenty-two cities five methods for securing attendance were found: (*a*) by reporting to state department, (*b*) by coördinators, (*c*) by special officers, (*d*) by regular attendance officers, (*e*) by special attendance department.[16] One city was obliged to report to a state department but used the regular public school attendance service. The two cities that reported the use of teachers or coördinators found this system more prompt and satisfactory than the use of the regular attendance department. It was claimed that the teachers and coördinators had a better understanding of the pupils than the truant officer had and obtained valuable information that was helpful in making better adjustments of the school work. It was also felt that where teachers and coördinators were actively engaged in the work their use for attendance cuts down the number of people from the school calling on the business man and added one more reason for a contact between school and business through the teaching staff.

Five cities provided a special officer attached to the regular attendance department but assigned to special work with part-time pupils. Eleven cities used the regular attendance officer. The results obtained were not in general satisfactory. It was claimed that the district was so large that the attendance officer could not become personally acquainted with the part-time absentees and it was also claimed that there were too many officers on the job.

Of the twenty-three cities four had a special attendance service independent of the regular department. All reported this method satisfactory.

The conclusion reached in the report was that it was impossible to offer specific recommendations for the use of any one method. Cities vary so much in size and are confronted with so many special local problems that each method should be noted and a city "use any of them at any time and for any purpose, as it is felt that one or another method will produce best results." [17]

Of the fifteen cities of this study nine were compelled to enforce part-time education laws. In all these cities the attendance depart-

16 Part-Time Schools, Bulletin No. 73, Federal Board of Vocational Education, p. 244.
17 *Ibid.,* p. 248.

ment was held responsible for investigating absences for which excuses had not been received. In no city was it possible to assign an officer to each school, the attendance department being too understaffed for such service. The schools investigated absences by telephone calls to the parent or employer wherever possible and reported to the attendance officer those who required his attention. Cities D and E took the drastic method of revoking employment certificates for continued illegal absence and announced the name in school as a warning to future would-be absentees. The revocation of permits was not practiced to any extent in the other cities.

Compulsory Evening Schools.—Few states require attendance upon evening school instruction for employed children of compulsory school age. "In four cities attendance upon evening instruction for a period of not less than the number of hours set in the part-time compulsory law is accepted, but the acceptance in three cases is largely restricted. It was authorized by law in only one city." [18]   For illiterates over the compulsory school age a "special" educational certificate was issued in Massachusetts.[19] "The holder of this certificate to be legally employed must present to his or her employer each week a record of his or her attendance in such school while a public evening school is maintained in the city or town in which the said holder resides."

This brings an added burden to the attendance department as shown in City A where 797, or approximately 7.1 per cent of the 11,211 cases of absences reported for the year, were of the evening school group and required 852 visits to homes.

CONCLUSIONS AND RECOMMENDATIONS

Some of the states have, in certain respects, passed beyond Massachusetts in the development of child labor laws and the protection of children, but all have at some time looked upon this state as the leader in the early battle against child labor and have patterned their laws after the methods prevailing in Massachusetts.[20]

In all the cities studied the same general procedure was accepted as desirable for obtaining employment certificates. If prac-

[18] *Ibid.,* p. 249.
[19] Massachusetts Department of Labor and Industries, Form J, 1923.
[20] Ensign, F. C., *Compulsory School Attendance and Child Labor,* p. 245.

tice had squared more generally with accepted theory we should have had the following procedure in force: (*a*) An application made by the child accompanied by the parent or guardian after the child had a definite (*b*) Promise of Employment and the necessity for such employment had been fully investigated by the attendance department. The child must then secure a (*c*) School Record certificate and offer (*d*) Documentary Proof of Physical Fitness based upon standards that will justify an employment certificate for work to be undertaken. After the child (*e*) has been registered in the continuation school where such schooling is required the (*f*) Certificate of Employment may be issued. This certificate should then be mailed to the employer-to-be and should be returned by mail immediately at the termination of employment.

It does not come within the scope of this study to give all the forms used in the enforcement of child labor laws. The forms required by state laws are as varied as the laws regarding child labor. Massachusetts alone, a large industrial state, has nine forms of employment certificates to meet the laws of the state. Certain records and reports, however, are necessary for safeguarding the interests of the child, the school, the employer and the state, and it is with such aims in mind that the following forms and records are recommended and described.

Form 53. Application for Employment.—Before an employment certificate is issued to a child the parent should present in person an application containing the following information:

1. Title, city and date of application.
2. Name of child for whom certificate is sought.
3. The age, sex, nationality, color, date of birth of child.
4. The age of other children in family.
5. The total estimated family income.
6. The school attended and grade.
7. Reasons for making application.
8. Prospective employer, the name and address.
9. Whether application is rejected or granted.
10. Where part-time school is compulsory, a statement that law is known.
11. Signature of parent.

Form 34. A Chronological Record of Applications.—Such a form should be kept and the following may be used:

FORM 54. RECORD OF APPLICATION

	CITY OF _____						
	RECORD OF APPLICATION FOR EMPLOYMENT CERTIFICATE						
DATE	NO. OF APPLICA-TION	NAME	ADDRESS	TYPE OF CERTI-FICATE	CLASSI-FICATION I-SI-S	GRANTED DATE	REJECTED DATE

The application blanks should be filed alphabetically until the employment papers are complete. They should then be filed with the other papers. In cities where there is a large foreign-born population it will be difficult to have these blanks (Form 53) filled out by the parent of the child.

Form 55. Promise of Employment.—In order to avoid the loss of school attendance due to a child's seeking employment after he has decided to leave school, the application for an employment certificate should be accompanied by a Promise of Employment from the prospective employer and should give:

1. City and title of form.
2. The factory number, if registered.
3. Name of child to whom employment is promised.
4. The age and sex of child.
5. The name of parent or guardian.
6. Address of parent or guardian.
7. The firm name or employer with address.
8. Specific nature of employment to which child is to be assigned.
9. The hours of employment and wages.
10. Quotations from state statutes regarding hours of labor.
11. Employer's promise to return employment certificate within two days (or legal requirement) after termination of employment.
12. Date, and signature of employer.

This form is filed in an envelope containing all of the child's employment forms as soon as a Card Record (Form 66) is complete.

Form 56. School Record Certificate.—The information required by this form will depend upon the state law. In general it should contain the following and should be filled out by the principal of the school the child last attended.

1. City and title of form.
2. Name, age, date of birth, sex, color, nationality.
3. Address of child.

4. Date of application for record.
5. Name of parent or guardian.
6. School and grade last attended.
7. Days in attendance during 12 months next preceding.
8. A statement that child has fulfilled educational requirements.
9. Signature of principal.

The School Record Certificate is easily printed in card form and in duplicate—the original to be retained at the issuing office and the duplicate to be returned to the school when the employment certificate is issued. No child should be discharged from school to enter employment until the duplicate has been received by the principal. On the back of the card should be the directions for issuing the School Record, a statement that an employment certificate has been issued, and the signature of the issuing officer.

Form 57. Proof of Age.—When a birth certificate, baptismal record, passport, immigration record or a certified true copy of baptism are not available, a physician's certificate of age and an affidavit of parent may be legally acceptable. The latter two should be as follows:

(*a*) Physician's Certificate of Age: [21]

FORM 57

PHYSICIAN'S CERTIFICATE OF AGE.   City of......................
Name of child
Place of birth   Date of birth
Address City   Street   State or Town   & No.
The undersigned hereby certifies that he—she—is unable to produce a birth certificate, baptismal certificate, passport, immigration record, an official or religious record, or school record, or a transcript of any of the aforesaid proofs of age of child named herein.

Town or City of	Signed
Signed in presence of	Parent
(for Supt. of schools)	Guardian Custodian

The undersigned hereby certifies that in his opinion the above-named child is at least fourteen to sixteen years of age.
Signature of _____   School Physician or Physician appointed by School Committee

[21] See Massachusetts Legal Form for Physician's Certificate of Age.

(*b*) Affidavit of Parent. It should contain:

1. Name of child, age and date of birth. No. of certificate.
2. Place of birth, sex, color, nationality.
3. Color of eyes, height, weight, distinguishing facial marks.
4. Present address.
5. Sworn statement of parent.
6. Address of parent.
7. Signature of notary.
8. Date.

Form 58. Age Certificate.—Where proof of age is returned to the child the "age certificate" shown on page 142 will serve as a permanent record that "proof of age" has been received. All Age Certificates should be filed alphabetically as they are a constant source of reference. Requests for duplicates are frequently necessary especially where the law requires their use by all minors seeking employment up to twenty-one years of age.

Form 59. Certificate of Employment.—The forms of the Certificate of Employment have been more completely developed in Massachusetts than may be found necessary in most states. The forms used are: (*a*) Employment Certificate, regular; (*b*) Employment Certificate, Non-resident; (*c*) Temporary; (*d*) Limited; (*e*) Home Employment Permit; (*f*) Special Employment; (*g*) Coöperative Employment; (*h*) Educational Certificate, regular for minors 16 to 21 who have fulfilled educational qualifications; (*i*) Educational Certificates, special for minors 16 to 21 who have not fulfilled educational requirements and must attend evening school.[22]

The more common practice, as indicated by the examination of state forms, is to have two kinds, the General Certificate and the Vacation Certificate. These two may be made to serve all purposes, unless the other forms are required by law. Whatever the form, it should be issued in duplicate, one copy for the office file and the other for the employer's file, to be returned by him to the attendance office immediately (2 days) after termination of employment. Every effort must be made to secure the coöperation of the employer in the enforcement of this requirement.

[22] See State Forms, Department of Labor and Industries, Massachusetts. **Form C-1923 to Form J-1923 inclusive.**

FORM 58. AGE CERTIFICATE

AGE CERTIFICATE | COMMONWEALTH OF PENNSYLVANIA
Department of Public Instruction
Attendance Bureau
Harrisburg

No........... ....Name of Minor
(Last name first)

Evidence of age accepted. (Cross out all except the one accepted.)
a. Birth Certificate.
b. Baptismal Certificate.
c. Passport.
d. Other documentary record.
e. Affidavit of Parent or Guardian accompanied by Physician's statement of opinion as to the age of minor.

Date of Birth		
Month	Day	Year

Signature of Minor...
(Name in full)

This is to certify that according to the records and above evidence of age filed in the office of the School District of..................the above-named minor is 16 years of age or over.

Issuing Officer.............................

Date........................... Position............................

[Reverse of Age Certificate]

TO THE EMPLOYER

This card is issued by the school district that the employer may have authentic evidence the minor is 16 years of age or over. It should be required by the employer of every minor not holding an employment certificate and employed since April 5, 1921, the date of the promulgation of ruling M-34 of the State Industrial Board. It should be kept on file while the minor is in his employ.

TO THE ISSUING OFFICER

The evidence of age indicated on the face of this certificate should be required in the order given. Insist upon a birth certificate if available, either from the parent or from the State Bureau of Vital Statistics, Harrisburg, Pennsylvania.

The best types of forms contain:

1. City and date of issue and type of certificate.
2. Number of certificate.
3. Factory number of place of employment.
4. Name of child, with age, sex, color, and color of eyes and hair.
5. Address, city, street, number, state.
6. Distinguishing facial marks.
7. School last attended, grade completed.
8. Employer, firm's name.
9. Business address of employer.
10. Evidence of age accepted: (*a*) birth certificate, (*b*) baptismal record, (*c*) passport or attested immigration, (*d*) physician's certificate, (*e*) other legal evidence.
11. Signature of child to whom certificate is granted.
12. Nature of employment.
13. Signature of attendance officer.
14. Statement that school record and physician's certificate of physical fitness have been filed.

(NOTE.—To be made in triplicate where State Department requires a copy.)

The reverse of card may be used for excerpts from the child labor laws regarding hours of employment, non-transferability of certificate, continuation school attendance, and responsibility of employer. The signature of parent or guardian may be required if desirable. All the information may be printed on a 4″ by 6″ card.

Form 60. Notice of Employment Certificate.—When an employment certificate for employment in another town or city is issued, the form shown on page 144 should be sent to the superintendent of schools of the other town or city.

Form 61. Notice of Employment Certificate and Receipt from Employer.—After an employment certificate has been issued for other than home employment, Form 61 should be sent to the employer and a receipt requested. It should be issued in return postal form as shown on page 144.

Form 62. Investigation for Home Permit.—Before home or employment certificates are issued regular investigations should be made. This form should be used for periodical investigations by the attendance officer and filed with the employment card. Such a form should show whether a permit should be issued or

FORM 60. NOTICE OF EMPLOYMENT CERTIFICATE

NOTICE OF EMPLOYMENT CERTIFICATE. City of......................

Date......................

To Supt. of Schools:

We are enclosing herewith a duplicate of an employment certificate, No.........issued...........................authorizing employment in your town (city) of....................................residing in ....
(city)

(name)

............................Signature of Att. Officer

City...................

(Please detach and return)

City or
Town........................ Date.......................

Received from attendance department...................duplicate of employment certificate, No........issued...................authorizing the employment in this town (city) of............................ whose residence is in................
(city)

(name)

....................................(Official Title)

FORM 61. NOTICE OF EMPLOYMENT CERTIFICATE AND RECEIPT FROM EMPLOYER

ATTENDANCE DEPARTMENT   City of...........................

Date..............................

To...................................

We have received a "Promise of Employment" signed by you agreeing to employ...(name) of...................................(address) Age......Boy—Girl. On...................................19....an employment certificate No.......was issued authorizing such employment. Will you please notify me on or before.......................19....if he—she does not enter your employ and oblige.

Yours very truly,

....
(Chief Attendance Officer)

....

(Return Postal Form)

ATTENDANCE DEPARTMENT   City of...........................
Date..............................

Dear Sir:

.... (name) ....(address) Age...... Boy—Girl entered (did not enter) our employ............ ....(address of employer)on......................192.... She—He will be employed.....hours at........................... ....(kind of employment) at.............wage.

Yours very truly,

....
(Signature of Employer)

the continuation of a permit justified. The form used in City A follows:

1. Name of child and address.
2. Father—where employed, wages............
3. Reason if not employed.
4. Mother—employed, since............wages............
5. Rent.
6. Other children—boys, girl.
7. Employed—wage............in school............
8. Younger children—boys, girls.
9. In school.
10. Reason for requesting home permit.
11. Remarks and recommendations.
12. Date, signature.

Regular checking of home employment is one of the most essential duties of the attendance service. It was reported in every city that many parents are found who are willing to exploit their children under the guise of necessary home employment.

Form 63. Application for Newsboy's Permit.—For those minors who apply for street employment certificates a special application form is required. A form that gives the information that should be required is given on page 146.[28]

These forms should be filed alphabetically and should show at all times the number of minors thus employed. The chronological list of Record of Employment Certificates (Form 65) will show the number issued during any period of time.

Form 64. Instructions for Street Trades.—Some cities find it desirable to issue instructions to boys who are authorized to engage in street trades. This form gives a statement of the state laws regarding such occupation and the requirements of the local board of education as to the badge to be worn and its return.

Form 65. Chronological List for Record of Certificates Issued.—This should give a record of all the different types of certificates issued, so arranged and classified that it is possible to give the total number of minors at work within the year. If the year is started with a known number of employed minors and the record of new certificates corrected during the year by maturing and lapsing certificates, it would give at any time the number of

[28] Form issued by Bureau of Attendance, New York City.

FORM 63. APPLICATION FOR NEWSBOY'S PERMIT

City of...................... Date..............................

APPLICATION OF PARENT AND PRINCIPAL FOR NEWSBOY'S PERMIT BADGE

| To Employment Certificating Officer .... | | 1 | to sell newspapers, periodicals, magazines .... | FOR |
| I hereby apply for a newsboy Permit Badge .... | | 2 | to distribute newspapers over a route .... | |

Family Name of Boy   Given Name   No.   Street
....

Born: Month.........Day......Yr......Birthplace..................
Color of hair............Color of eyes...........Distinguishing facial
marks..........................Signature of Parent.................

School Record of Boy

I hereby certify that...............................above described
is.......years of age, according to the records of this school, having
been born.........................19...., and that he is now attending
this school, and is of the normal development of a child of his age,
and physically fit for such employment, and I also apply for the issuance
of a permit badge to such child.
.....................................Prin. P.S......

Date	Height	Weight	APPLICATION		No. of Permit Badge	Badge Returned
			Granted	Refused		

(Signature of Boy)   (Employment Certificating Officer)

[*Reverse of Card*]

DESCRIPTION OF NEWSPAPER ROUTE

....
....
....

employed minors of all ages. The chronological list may take the following form:

FORM 65. RECORD OF EMPLOYMENT CERTIFICATES

Record of Employment Certificates. City of................... Year.........														
Date of Issue	Certificate No.	Name	Address	Type								Age-Group		
				A		B		C	D			14		15
				I-SI-S		I-SI-S		I-SI-S	I-SI-S		I-SI-S	I-SI-S		I-SI-S
Total this month														
Previous total														
Grand Total														

The types, A, B, C, D, and the distribution by age should be those required by law. Other types and ages may be added if desired.[24]

If separate records for boys and girls are necessary, differently colored record forms may be used. All certificates should be classified under one of three heads: I-Issue, the first certificate issued for the given year to a minor; SI-New Certificate, of another form issued to the same minor; S-Subsequent Certificate, of same form issued to the same minor in that year. The grand total resulting from the sum of columns I, SI, and S gives the total number of certificates issued. The values in the age-groups give a check upon the record of the types of certificates issued.

Form 66. Record of Employment.—A card file may be used for this record or it may be kept on the envelope used for filing all employment papers. This record as it appears on the portfolio of employment papers gives all the information necessary.

FORM 66. RECORD OF EMPLOYMENT

Record of Employment. City of.....................				
Name....................... Certificate No.......... Address............St.......No. Date of birth,Mo....Day....Yr.. Parent.................... Place of birth................. School.........Grade.....Proof of age.....................				
Started	Left	Remarks	Employed by	Salary

[24] See Massachusetts Forms for Educational Certificates, Forms I and J, 1923.

Form 67.   Notice to Continuation School and Report of Registration.—As soon as the child has completed all the requirements necessary for the issuance of an employment certificate a notice should be sent with the child to the continuation school notifying the principal that the issuance of an employment certificate awaits the child's registration in his school.   Such a notice should give:

1. City.
2. Name of child, date of birth, sex, color, nationality.
3. Date of issue, number, type and classification of certificate.
4. Parent or guardian.
5. Nationality and occupation of parent or guardian.
6. Last school attended and grade.
7. Name of employer.
8. Address of employer.

On the reverse of the card should be:

9. Statement of continuation school law.
10. Signature of pupil.
11. Day in continuation school.
12. Date of entry.
13. Signature of principal of continuation school.

When this card is returned from the continuation school it should be filed alphabetically for an easy reference file of employment records.   A file for employed, unemployed, and out-of-town cases for active cards is desirable.   If the attendance department requires the signature of the continuation school principal in other communities where the child is employed, serious loss will be avoided in states like New Jersey and Massachusetts.   In these states the child attends continuation school where he is employed, not where he resides and obtains his employment certificate.   A numerical portfolio file should be kept of all the legal forms required for the issuance of employment certificates.   In this way a "live file" and a "dead file" may be accessible for all employment certificates issued.   Reference to these files may be by number from the card file of Form 67.

Form 68.   Notice to Employer.—When a child is enrolled in the continuation school a notice should be sent to the employer giving him the day and hours the child will be required to attend. In one city the Promise of Employment (Form 55) contained a space where the employer could indicate any preference he might have regarding hours of attendance.

FORM 68. NOTICE TO EMPLOYER

CONTINUATION SCHOOL.

City of...........................

NOTICE TO EMPLOYER.

Name of Employer....................................
This is to notify you that..,
a minor between......and......years of age, employed by you must attend this school on..............................from...........
to.................
Signed.................................Prin.

Form 69. Notice of Change of Attendance.—A similar notice should be used when it becomes necessary to change the time of attendance.

FORM 69. NOTICE OF CHANGE OF ATTENDANCE

CONTINUATION SCHOOL. City of...........................

NOTICE OF CHANGE OF ATTENDANCE

Name of Employer....................................
This is to notify you that.......................................,
a minor between......and...... years of age, employed by you, has had his—her hours of attendance changed from............and...........
to............and............
Signed.................................Prin.

Form 70. Pupil Attendance Record for Employer.—In order that the employer may have a regular report from the school that the employee has been in attendance, the form shown on page 150 can be used. When the employer pays for the time in school, as many do, he is entitled to have a record of the attendance of the pupil.

Form 71. Make-up Record.—It is often necessary for pupils to be excused from attendance on the regular day assigned. Employers occasionally request such permission owing to some emergency. The coöperation and good-will of the employer is improved by honoring these requests when they are made so as to avoid loss of time in investigation by the attendance department

FORM 70.   PUPIL ATTENDANCE RECORD FOR EMPLOYER

City of............																			

Pupil Attendance Record for Employer.

1	2	3	4	5	6	7	8	9	10	11	12	13	14	15	16	17	18	19	20
September				October				November			December					January			

School Yr. 192..-192.	PART-TIME SCHOOL
SHOW THIS CARD TO YOUR EMPLOYER	This card certifies that the bearer whose signature appears below, is registered at the Part-Time School in accordance with sec.601 of the Educational Law and has attended as required for the weeks punched P.T.

Pupil.................   ....Dir.

February				March				April				May				June			
1	2	3	4	5	6	7	8	9	10	11	12	13	14	15	16	17	18	19	20

or the school. As in the case of other absences these absences should be made up.

Experience shows that poor attendance is the result of failure to require that absence on any one day of the week be made up the same week. A notice to the teacher of the date when such time is to be made up may take the following form: [25]

FORM 71.   MAKE-UP RECORD

MAKE-UP RECORD		City of..........................			

Date......................   Teacher..........................

....is to make up time as follows:

(Pupils to attend all sessions cancelled)

	Date	8–10	10–12	1–3	3–5	
Mon..		8–10	10–12	1–3	3–5	
Tues..		8–10	10–12	1–3	3–5	
Wed..		8–10	10–12	1–3	3–5	
Thurs.		8–10	10–12	1–3	3–5	
Fri...		8–10	10–12	1–3	3–5	
Sat...		8–10	10–12	1–3	3–5	

As time is made up check each period with your initials in blank space following hours and return this slip to office when schedule has been completed. If pupil does not appear on date specified, return unchecked.

.....................................Director

[25] See Form 21, Buffalo, N. Y.

FORM 72. INDIVIDUAL ATTENDANCE RECORD

CONTINUATION SCHOOL   City of...........................

Name..........................Date enrolled......................
Employment Certificate No.......Will be sixteen....................
Address........................Date of birth......................
Parent or   Nationality........................
Guardian......................Occupation.........................
Last School Attended..................................Grade......
Reason for leaving.......................Left......................
Vocational Preference...

Date	Employer	Address	Kind of Work	Wage

Reason for changing employment.....................................
Reason for leaving Continuation School.............................
Date..

[*Reverse of Form 72*]

ATTENDANCE RECORD

Name...   Day......................

	Sept.	Oct.	Nov.	Dec.	Jan.
Wk.					
192...A.M					
P.M.					

	Feb.	Mar.	Apr.	May	June
Wk.					
192. .A.M.					
P.M.					

	Sept.	Oct.	Nov.	Dec.	Jan.
Wk.					
192 A.M					
P M					

	Feb	Mar	Apr	May	June
Wk					
192...A.M.					
P.M.					

Summary

Possible Hours	Actual Hours	Hours Absent	Times Tardy	Per Cent Attendance
1st yr. 2nd	1st 2nd	1st 2nd	1st 2nd	1st 2nd yr.

Indicate—Present (P), Tardy (T), Absent (A), Entered (E), Out (O).

Form 72. Individual Attendance Record.—Although the attendance forms heretofore described may be used for reporting absences and keeping attendance records, it is often desirable to keep a complete daily attendance record on one card for the duration of the child's continuation school life. This may be a permanent record card such as the form shown on page 151.

Graphic Chart of Employment Certificates.—A graphic chart showing the number of certificates issued each month to boys and girls, if regularly maintained, will give a picture of the child employment conditions over a period of years and will present a valuable picture of the labor conditions.

In offering the above records and reports it is constantly borne in mind that none should be included which will not actually be utilized in the school system. Wherever possible the composition of these forms has been determined by current practice of the most efficiently organized attendance departments, with the endeavor to overcome the acknowledged shortcomings of the cities studied.

The utility of any or all of these forms will be somewhat dependent upon the legal requirements of the state, but an endeavor has been made to adapt them to recognized legal and educational standards so that any city desiring to give an informing accounting of its attendance stewardship will have, in the plans outlined, a basis of such an accounting that it will offer enlightening records for the advancement of the best educational interests of the child and the community.

CHAPTER VII

CONCLUSION

"No field in education with the possible exception of school revenues has in recent years been more prolific of progress as regards legislative provisions than has compulsory school attendance."[1] It is true that there has been a steady country-wide increase with the per cent of children enrolled attending school each day, the average number of days schools were in session, as well as the average number of years of two hundred days that children remain in school. The last of the states that had not enacted laws have finally made some attempt to meet their attendance problem.

With all the good work that has been done, the commissioner of education is compelled to comment on the fact that such a large part of our population are without the pale of the schools that it imperils the future of this country.[2]

Too often the public has been satisfied with the enactment of legislation based, at the time, on sentiment and public opinion, but the burden of providing the necessary machinery and making it imperative has been overlooked or cast aside.

One who examines closely the attendance conditions in our cities must feel that the inner workings of the administrative machinery and the conditions revealed are deplorable. Those in the school system are aware of the shortcomings and seem anxious to improve them, but little technical assistance has as yet been offered to them either in scientific studies of the field or in the offering of opportunities for training in this field of labor.

Cities are found, like City K of our study, where lists of "readings" have been prepared and the literature of the special problems and those in the allied fields of sociology and psychology assigned for study and discussion. Such attempts give evidence of a new outlook for attendance service.

[1] U. S. Commissioner of Education, Report, 1920, p. 77.
[2] N.E.A., Department of Superintendents, "Ideals of Public Education," p. 16.

SCHOOL CENSUS AND SCHOOL ATTENDANCE

The school census must form the basis of the child accounting of the schools, the enforcement of school attendance and the child labor laws. With the census inaccurate, incomplete and not up-to-date no true accounting can be made of the children illegally out of school, the children so handicapped that they need special instruction, and the children who are employed. With a continuing or live census a complete list of all children who are amenable to the compulsory education law is always available for the attendance worker. Modern child accounting must not stop short of any possibility to discover the items of information needed. It is as necessary for the school as it is for an industrial plant to know, by an examination of its books, its assets and liabilities.

States now generally set forth in their laws the information desired concerning each child enumerated, but there is no recognized effort to secure an accounting of the child from birth throughout his minority. The home is not a mere preliminary to the school nor are the child's years from the close of the compulsory school period, with its contributions to physical, intellectual and moral growth, to his majority, without concern to society. No full measure of meeting the future outlook for society's oversight of the child can be secured without the complete continuing census of the child population from birth to twenty-one years.

RELATION OF PUBLIC AND NON-PUBLIC SCHOOLS TO ATTENDANCE SERVICE

In all the cities studied the lack of full coöperation of the non-public schools made the attendance service, even that legally required, apparently impossible of attainment. The so-called continuing census of all the cities broke down and became the mere registration of public school pupils. Losses are too serious to be longer neglected. Coöperation must be built up to a point where the state knows that all the children are in attendance. The question of state regulation and supervision will become constantly more serious if the standards in this study are to be attained. The state cannot claim that it has performed its duty toward all its citizens if it does not know all the children in all the schools and if it does not safeguard their attendance and employment.

THE STATE AND NATION IN ATTENDANCE SERVICE

Education and industry present two inseparable groups of problems. In both the state has in many instances asserted its supremacy by constantly extending the degree of compulsory education and by the prohibition and restriction of child labor.

Many who see in our country more than a federation of sovereign states believe that our conception of education has been narrow and provincial. Although brought together primarily for common defense we have gradually widened our interests in the general welfare and progress of the nation as a whole. Some, as would be expected, have looked upon this widening interest as a threat to our democratic institutions. For them it has been the result of designing and partisan individuals rather than the expression of a deep and pressing need.[3]

One who comes into constant personal contact with the attendance policies of our different states and communities cannot fail to be impressed with the evident lack of some strong unifying force. The price we pay as a people for local responsibility in education is plainly written in the administration and organization of school attendance in every state in the Union. The war crisis revealed much that was not a source of pride. Here and there from time to time a state or community school survey discloses the true educational conditions, and yet we go on as if each hamlet may have its own ideals and standards heedless of the fact that it is no longer isolated but a part of one big "neighborhood which is no smaller than the nation." [4]

States are slowly proceeding in the direction of more complete control of education. All have adjusted themselves to a wider control of child labor than of school attendance. Connecticut has more fully committed herself to a state[5] administration of both child labor and attendance than has any other state. New York[6] and Pennsylvania,[7] where the state authorities have the power to penalize the local committees for the failure to comply with the regulations, have not succeeded in providing the necessary supervision of attendance service. This was shown by the conditions

[3] Keith, J. A. H. and Bagley, W. C., *The Nation and the School*, pp. 1-7.
[4] *Ibid.*, p. 3.
[5] Children's Bureau Publication No. 12, p. 51.
[6] New York Laws of 1894, Chap. 671.
[7] Pennsylvania State Laws of 1922.

of the census and attendance in the cities of those states in our study. Both of these states require an honest, fearless administration to give to them a position of leadership to which their laws entitle them.

Whether or not the national authorities must intervene in attendance service remains to be seen. In child labor there is a determination on the part of many that the national government must coöperate in fixing national standards and enforcing requirements. As a people we are interested not solely in our particular state but in the citizenship of our common country. When a nation-wide study of attendance service is made the necessity for a greater national interest in securing the regular attendance of every child upon a school day of minimum educational standards will be evident.

More thoroughgoing state supervision of continuing census and school attendance is desirable and necessary if the local communities are to be brought to standards that should be expected. When the local school authorities rather than the state authorities enumerate the school population and report on the degree to which the task of regular attendance of all the school population is attained, there is serious danger that the enumeration will not always show the failure of the school authorities to meet their obligations.

THE CHANGING CONCEPTION OF ATTENDANCE SERVICE

From the early conception of attendance service with its highly emphasized police functions we have gradually developed the modern conception that true attendance service will recognize the place of compulsion but at all times will place the welfare of the child first. Experience and change in social demands have brought the mere checking of truancy and irregularity of attendance into disrepute. Police methods are now inadequate and often inappropriate. The method should be the discovery and elimination of causes. A prevention by striking at the cause is more important than an attempt to cure.

School administrators, recognizing the futility of forcing the child into school by threats of the law, have begun to provide the means to determine physical and mental conditions through their physical and mental health clinics. The relief of needy pupils by donations of worn clothing from pupils and the "shoe funds" and scholarships is now found to be a prominent welfare activity of attendance departments.

The broken home and its resulting school ills are often more difficult to solve, but the visiting teacher and the special workers through their coöperation with the other welfare agencies find it possible to place the child in a better environment. A significant evidence of the change that is taking place in the attendance service is the plea, made from time to time, that the official titles of the department and its personnel be changed to conform to the new type of social service performed by them.[8]

An outstanding example of the change that has taken place is seen in Cincinnati where public and private agencies are working together in a vocational bureau that includes most of the recognized child-accounting policies. One third of the expense is borne by private agencies.

The objectives of modern attendance should be:

1. To secure an accurate continuing census as a basis for the enforcement of attendance and child labor laws.
2. To keep all children in school by removing the causes of absence, by securing medical or nursing aid and by providing food, clothing or scholarship.
3. To help solve the children's problems. It believes that the more it knows about the child, his home, his environments and his mental and physical peculiarities, the better it can serve the child and the school.
4. To supervise young workers in industry.
5. To study the delinquent child before he is brought into court and endeavor to reform him if there is any way open to success in this endeavor.
6. To determine the true causes of truancy and to bring all the social and educational facilities of the community to meet the needs of the individual child.

COST OF ATTENDANCE SERVICE

Studies have been made to find what factors in school attendance service are related to the cost of enforcement. Little or no

[8] Gideon, H. J., Annual Report, Philadelphia, 1920, p. 7.

correlation seems to exist in any of the factors analyzed, such as percentage of attendance, parents arrested, health service, percentage of native-born whites, population per capita wealth. "The character of the service rendered is more directly related to the salary cost per child than to any other factor." [9]

Costs will be increased by the changing ideals of service, as shown by the greater use of school nurses, special workers, visiting teachers, psychologists, and attendance officers whose educational background is in keeping with the requirements of social service rather than the ability to do good police, detective and enforcement duty.

The cost must rise as school authorities recognize more generally that the preventive service requires a more highly trained and numerous personnel than was needed for the mere notice and messenger service that prevailed so exclusively in the past. From the recent city surveys the per capita cost of the attendance service as determined by the local distribution of costs does not include estimates of all the costs of the new services that are being added. In cities of New York State the per capita cost was in general less than one per cent of the per pupil cost for total expenses.

The salary of the attendance officer is the chief expenditure. The upper limit of per pupil attendance cost in all cities of the state was 94 cents with a median for all cities of 23 cents per pupil. From such data and that previously given from the cities studied an accurate estimate of the cost of adequate attendance service would be more or less futile.

Cities are now employing visiting teachers, school visitors, co-ordinators and home visitors, most of them professionally trained. These often taken up the work of the attendance officer at the point where for lack of education and training he is no longer of service. Attendance officers with the qualifications for professional service must receive salaries commensurate with the service rendered.

With one attendance officer for three thousand pupils of compulsory school age and one clerk for every two or three officers, as the local conditions may demand, the salaries alone paid for the type of officers and clerical help needed should bring the salary

[9] Hanson, W. L., *Cost of Compulsory Attendance Service in the State of New York,* Chapter VIII.

budget to not less than one dollar per pupil. Few cities are as yet expending this amount. Each city, however, must draw into the service those whose qualifications of general education, special training and experience will enable them to gain a sympathetic attitude towards the social and economic problems of the family and those who have an understanding of the principles of child psychology, the work of the school room, case work technique and the many problems of school attendance service.

The immediate cost of securing and training the attendance personnel for the performance of the type of service recommended will be greater than the estimated costs in any of the cities now recognized as leaders in the type of attendance service offered, but the ultimate cost to the state and the community will be less if by such service the child's education is safeguarded and he becomes a more desirable social asset.

THE OUTLOOK

Educational literature in the field of school administration is gradually disclosing to school authorities the necessity for more adequate child accounting. Financial and cost accounting are necessary but all must be subordinated to the satisfaction of the child's educational needs. When these needs are made the object of scientific research then school attendance or the contact of the child with the educational offerings is directly or indirectly involved.

Agencies outside the schools are at work endeavoring to aid the school authorities to meet the difficult problems of child life in which the school plays so important a part. They are beginning to recognize that burdens that once belonged elsewhere have been thrust upon the school. To accomplish the many difficult tasks trained and experienced workers are needed. School administrators can no longer hope to perform a satisfactory service unless they are trained for their special task. "In Service Training" is now deemed necessary to raise the standards of every profession, and the attendance service must have provisions for such training. The state has not yet placed any minimum requirements for the attendance officer and the type of service so long required did not demand that it should.

To take an accurate census, to maintain it, to establish relations with the home, to know the social agencies in the community, and to be a part of their activities, requires more training than was needed for the old type of "truant officer." The new type must be a social worker who will seek to coördinate the home, the school and the community by an understanding and experience which such a profession demands. This work should no longer be a job handed out to some needy political friend, but a profession with qualifications, standards and salary commensurate with the duties to be assumed.

Conscious effort in the study of actual attendance service conditions will awaken school authorities to the fact that our present child accounting does not enable us to say that we have fully safeguarded every future citizen in his right to a training for a useful part in the life of the nation.

Zealous, high-minded attendance officers, with their national organization, and far-sighted school superintendents are seeking ways and means whereby the present level of attendance service may be raised. City surveys bring before the people the present weaknesses and also call their attention to the objectives of the best administered departments which are endeavoring to insure the community a full and efficient use of the school plant and to safeguard society by keeping the child in punctual and regular attendance upon instruction. They show how some seek to insure the child the fullest opportunity of the school by adjusting his education to his ability and needs and to prevent delinquency by a sympathetic study of the child. Others must sooner or later follow. By counseling the child worker in his endeavor to become a producer in life and by lending a hand to the ambitious child handicapped by the economic pressure at home, the attendance service assumes responsibilities in keeping with present social requirements.

Such a program is now enlisting the best thought of school administrators, educators and social workers. The future, however, must not be left to the individual initiative of scattered enthusiasts or far-sighted administrators. It must be assumed by all the states—as it already has been by some—as one of the most important functions that the state can assume in the endeavor to safeguard its citizenry.

BIBLIOGRAPHY

ABBOTT, EDITH and BRECKENRIDGE, SOPHONISHA. *Truancy and Non-Attendance in Chicago Schools.* Chicago, Ill., University of Chicago Press, 1917.

ALABAMA, DEPARTMENT OF EDUCATION. (Bulletin No. 57.) *Compulsory School Attendance, Effective October 1, 1917.* The Law. Suggestions for Its Interpretation and Enforcements. Specimen Forms. Montgomery, Alabama. Department of Education, 1917.

American Child, The. Vol. VII. New York City, January, 1925.

ANTHONY, JOHN W. "Compulsory Education in Pennsylvania." In Pennsylvania State Education Association, Department of City and Borough Superintendents, *Proceedings,* 1910, pp. 11-18. Also in *Pennsylvania School Journal,* 58: 481-88, May, 1910.

Atlanta Survey. Board of Education, Atlanta, Georgia, 1922.

AYRES, LEONARD P. "Money Cost of Non-Attendance." *Proceedings,* Second Annual Educational Congress, pp. 35-37, November 11, 13, 1920.

AYRES, LEONARD P. *Child Accounting in the Public Schools, Cleveland, Ohio.* The Survey Committee of the Cleveland Foundation, 1915.

AYRES, LEONARD P. "Index of State School Systems." See *Research Bulletin of the N.E.A.,* Vol. I, No. 4, September, 1923.

AYRES, LEONARD P. *Laggards in Our Schools.* New York, Survey Associates, Inc., 1913.

BACHMAN, FRANK P. *Problems in Elementary School Administration.* Yonkers, N. Y., World Book Co., 1916.

Baltimore Survey. Vol. 2. Board of Education, Baltimore, Md., 1922.

BERMEJO, F. V. *The School Attendance Service in American Cities.* Menasha, Wis., George Banta Publishing Co., 1923.

BERMEJO, F. V. "The Permanent Continuing School Census." *American School Board Journal,* Vol. 65, December, 1922, No. 6, p. 43. Milwaukee, Wis., The Bruce Publishing Co.

BIRKELO, C. P. "A Complete Census, Its Functions and Value." *American School Board Journal,* Vol. 65, No. 5, p. 76.

BIXLER, EDWARD CLINTON. *An Investigation to Determine the Efficiency with Which the Compulsory Attendance Law Is Enforced.* Philadelphia, University of Pennsylvania, 1913.

BODINE, W. L. "Throwing the Burden of Truancy on the Parents." *Charities,* 17: 535-36, Dec. 22, 1906.

161

BONNER, H. R. "The Conviction of Legislators for Failure to Enact Effective Compulsory Attendance Laws." *American School Board Journal,* February, 1923.

BONNER, H. R. "Waste in Education." *American School Board Journal,* 63: 33-35, 124, July, 1921.

BONNER, H. R. "Persistence in Attendance in City Schools." *School Life,* 5: 10-11, October, 1920.

BOONE, RICHARD G. "Compulsory School Attendance." In his *Education in the United States.* New York, D. Appleton and Co., 1890. Pp. 326-31; Bibliography, pp. 330-31.

BRECKENRIDGE, S. P. and ABBOTT, EDITH. *The Delinquent Child and the Home.* New York, Charities Organization Committee, 1912.

BURKS, JESSE D. "The Compulsory Attendance Service." In New York City Committee on School Inquiry of the Board of School Estimates and Apportionment, *Interim Report, Educational Aspects of the Public School System.* New York, 1911-12.

BUREAU OF EDUCATION, Washington, D. C. Bonner, H. R. Bulletin No. 11, 1918. Bulletin No. 2, Compulsory School. Attendance, 1914. Bulletin No. 29, 1915. Bulletin No. 22, 1922. Bulletin No. 29, 1922. Bulletin No. 34, 1921-22.

Butte, Montana, Survey. Pp. 52-59. Yonkers, N. Y., World Book Co., 1916.

CARROLL, CHARLES. "The Supreme Court and Compulsory Education." *American School Board Journal,* Vol. 68, No. 5, p. 47, May, 1924.

CHATFIELD, GEORGE H. "What Provisions Should a Compulsory Education Law Include from the Point of View of Aim and Viewpoint of Enforcement?" In *Journal of the National Education Association,* Vol. I, No. 10, 1917.

"Child Labor." *Congressional Record,* Vol. 65, No. 90, No. 114 to 119, No. 128, No. 156. Washington, D. C., 1924.

CHILDREN'S BUREAU—and Other Publications Relating to Children—List of Publications relating to above subjects for sale by the Supt. of Documents, Washington, D. C., Bulletin No. 12; No. 17, No. 41, No. 85.

CINCINNATI, THE VOCATION BUREAU. Cincinnati Public Schools, Cincinnati, Ohio, 1922.

Compulsory Part-Time School, The. Bulletin No. 212. Michigan State Board of Control for Vocational Education, 1921.

CONNECTICUT, BOARD OF EDUCATION. *Attendance Agents, Study of Their Activities for the Year 1918-19.* (n. p.) 1919. State Board of Education, Statistical Studies, 1st series, 1919-20.

COOK, W. A. "A Brief Survey of the Development of Compulsory Education in the United States." *Elementary School Teacher,* 12: 331-35, March, 1912.

CUBBERLEY, ELLWOOD P. *Public Education in the United States.* New York, Houghton Mifflin Co., 1920.

DAVIS, JOHN W. "The Work of the New York Bureau of Compulsory Attendance." *American School Board Journal,* 53: 22, 667, December, 1916.

DAVIS, JOHN W. *First Annual Report of the Director of Attendance for Year Ending July 31st, 1915.* New York City Board of Education, 1916.

DAVIS, JOHN W. "The Need of a Continuing Census of Children of School Age." *National Education Association, Addresses and Proceedings,* p. 665, 1918. "The Taking of the School Census." *National Education Association, Addresses and Proceedings,* p. 496, 1915.

DENVER PUBLIC SCHOOLS. Monograph No. 8. *Organization and Work of the Department of Census and Attendance, 1924.*

DETROIT PUBLIC SCHOOLS. *Annual Report, Board of Education, 1923.*

DIETRICH, MARION C. "Attendance in High Schools." *Intermountain Educator,* 16: 51-54, October, 1920.

DORR, R. C. "New Method of Handling School Truants." *Hampton,* 26: 77-78, January, 1911.

DRAPER, ANDREW S. *Conserving Childhood.* New York City, Pamphlet No. 100. National Child Labor Committee, 1923.

DUTTEN, S. and SNEDDEN, DAVID. "Compulsory Education and Child Labor Legislation." In their *The Administration of Public Education in the United States.* New York, The Macmillan Co., 1908. (New Ed., 1912.)

ELLWOOD, CHARLES A. "Our Compulsory Education Laws." *Education,* 34, May, 1914.

ENGELHARDT, FRED. *Forecasting School Population.* New York, Teachers College, Columbia University, 1924.

ENGELHARDT, N. L. *A School Building Program for Cities.* Part 1. New York, Teachers College, Columbia University, 1918.

ENSIGN, FOREST CHESTER. *Compulsory School Attendance and Child Labor. A Study of the Historical Development of Regulations Compelling Attendance and Limiting the Labor of Children in a Selected Group of States.* New York, Teachers College, Columbia University, 1921.

EVENDEN, EDWARD SAMUEL. *Teachers' Salaries and Salary Schedules in the United States, 1918-1919.* Prepared for the Commission on the Emergency in Education of the National Education Association, Washington, D. C., 1919.

FEDERAL BOARD OF VOCATIONAL EDUCATION. *Part-Time Schools.* Bulletin No. 73. Washington, D. C., 1922.

FIESER, J. L. "The Attendance Officer as an Interpreter of Social Forces." *Educational Review,* 43: 80-85, January, 1912.

FOLKS, GERTRUDE. "Farm Labor vs. School Attendance." *American Child,* Vol. II, 73-89, May, 1920.

FULKS, B. F. "The Cumulative School Census in the Small City." *American School Board Journal,* Vol. 67, No. 3, September, 1923.

FULLER, RAYMOND G. *Child Labor and the Constitution.* New York, Thomas Y. Crowell Co., 1923.

GIDDINGS, F. H. Compulsory Education and Child Labor, the Social and Legal Aspect. *National Education Association, Addresses and Proceedings,* pp. 11-13, 1905.

GIDEON, HENRY J. *Report of Bureau of Compulsory Education.* Philadelphia, Pa., Walther Printing House, 1924.

GREESON, WILLIAM A. "The School Census and Its Use in School Administration." *Elementary School Journal,* Vol. XIX, September, 1918.

GRIFFEN, JOSEPH T. "Causes of Truancy." *Report of Superintendent of Schools, New York,* 1912.

GULICK, LUTHER HALSEY and AYRES, LEONARD P. *Medical Inspection of Schools.* New York, Russell Sage Foundation, 1917.

HABENS, PAUL B. "The Factors of an Adequate School Census. How They May Be Realized." *Journal of the National Education Association,* Vol. I, pp. 1063-1065, June, 1917.

HALL, BERT. "Truancy, a Few Cases and a Few Cures." In *National Education Association, Addresses and Proceedings,* pp. 217-22, 1909.

HALLOCK, HENRY GALLOWAY. *Compulsory Education, Do We Need It?* Princeton, N. J., Princeton University Press, 1896.

HAND, W. H. "The Need of Compulsory Education in the South." In *Conference for Education in the South, Proceedings,* pp. 55-70, 1912.

HANEY, JOHN DEARLING. *Registration of City School Children.* New York, Teachers College, Columbia University, 1910.

HANSON, WHITTIER LORENZ. *The Costs of Compulsory Attendance Service in the State of New York and Some Factors Affecting the Cost.* New York, Teachers College, Columbia University, 1924.

HANUS, PAUL H. "The Compulsory Attendance Service in New York City." Committee on School Inquiry, Excerpt from the Report as a Whole, New York, 1911-12.

HANUS, PAUL H. *School Administration and School Reports.* New York, Houghton Mifflin Co., 1920.

HANUS, PAUL H. *School Efficiency.* Yonkers, N. Y., World Book Co.

HARRIS, WILLIAM T. "Compulsory Education in Relation to Crime and Social Morals." In *U. S. Bureau of Education, Report of the Commissioner for the Year 1898-99.* Vol. II, 1311-18.

HARTWELL, S. O. "The Administration of Compulsory Attendance Laws." *National Education Association, Addresses and Proceedings,* p. 485, 1915.

HAYS, J. G. "Compulsory Education Law with Some Adverse Criticism." *Pennsylvania School Journal,* 54: 397-403, March, 1906.

HECK, A. O. In *Educational Research Bulletin,* Vol. III, pp. 298-303, October 29, 1924.

HECK, A. O. *The Status of Child Accounting Records and the Selection of Items for a Child Accounting System, Columbus, Ohio.* Bureau of Educational Research, Monograph No. 2, Ohio State University, 1924.

HENRY, MRS. A. C. "A Mother Truant Officer." *American School Board Journal,* 67: 32, 123, October, 1923.

HERVEY, HENRY D. "Compulsory Education and the Child Labor Law. Is Additional Legislation Needed?" *American Education,* 15: 256-60, February, 1912.

HIATT, JAMES S. *The Child, the School and the Job.* Philadelphia, Public Education Association, Study No. 39, 1912.

HIATT, JAMES S. *The Truant Problem and the Parental School.* U. S. Bureau of Education, Bulletin No. 29, 1915.

HISER, P. N. "Compulsory Education in Relation to the Charity Problem." In *Conference of Charities and Corrections,* pp. 277-85, 1900.

HOCHFELDER, JULIUS. *Attendance Officer Examination Instruction. Truant Officer. 450 Questions and Answers.* New York, Civil Service Chronicle, 1914.

IRWIN, ELIZABETH A. *Truancy, A Study of the Mental, Physical and Social Factors of the Problem of Non-Attendance at Schools.* New York City, Public Education Association, June, 1915.

JERNEGAN, MARCUS W. "Compulsory Education in the American Colonies." *School Review,* December, 1918.

JUDD, CHARLES H. *The Evolution of a Democratic School System.* New York, Houghton Mifflin Co., 1918.

KEITH, JOHN A. H. and BAGLEY, WILLIAM C. *The Nation and the Schools.* New York, Macmillan Co., 1920.

KELLER, FRANKLIN J. "Day Schools for Young Workers." New York, The Century Co., 1924.

KELLEY, FLORENCE M. "Laws for the Children's Welfare." In *National Education Association, Addresses and Proceedings,* pp. 1222-28, 1908.

KENNEDY, J. B. "Compulsory Education." *Elementary School Teacher,* 13: 315-56, March, 1913.

Know and Help Your Schools. Bulletin No. 2. New York, American City Bureau, 1921.

LORD, EVERETT W. *Child Labor and Public Schools.* New York, Publications of the National Child Labor Committee, 1900.

LOVEJOY, OWEN R. "The Function of Education in Abolishing Child Labor." In *National Child Labor Committee Proceedings, 1908,* pp. 180-91, New York, 1908.

MARTIN, G. H. "Compulsory Education and Child Labor. The School Aspect." In *National Education Association, Addresses and Proceedings,* pp. 103-11, 1905.

MENGEL, MRS. HERBERT W. "Compulsory School Attendance in the South." In *National Education Association, Addresses and Proceedings,* pp. 1229-31, 1908.

MILTON, GEORGE F. "Compulsory Education." In *National Child Labor Committee Proceedings, 1908,* pp. 57-66, New York, 1908.

MOEHLMAN, ARTHUR B. *Child Accounting: A Discussion of the General Principles Underlying Educational Child Accounting together with the Development of a Uniform Procedure.* Detroit, Mich., Friesema Bros. Press, 1924.

MONROE, PAUL. "Attendance—Compulsory." *Cyclopedia of Education,* Vol. I, pp. 285-95. New York, Macmillan Co., 1912.

MOORE, ERNEST CARROLL. "Effect of Compulsory Education on the Poor." Western Journal of Education, 7: 33-45, June, 1902.

MOORE, ERNEST CARROLL. "Compulsory Education: Report to the Council of Education on the Need of Compulsory Education Law in California." *Western Journal of Education,* 8: 65-77, February, 1903.

MORGAN, L. P. "The School Census." *American School Board Journal.* Vol. 64, No. 3, p. 44, March, 1922.

MORRISON, H. C. "Attendance Division." In *Survey of St. Louis Public Schools,* by Charles H. Judd. Yonkers, N. Y., World Book Co., 1918.

NATIONAL CHILD LABOR COMMITTEE. "Child Labor Laws in All States. Summary." *Child Labor Bulletin,* Vol. I, No. 2, pp. 1-77, August, 1912. (Includes Education Provision.) *The American Child,* Vol. VII, January, 1925.

NATIONAL EDUCATION ASSOCIATION. "Ideals of Public Education." P 16, 1922.

NATIONAL EDUCATION ASSOCIATION. *Research Bulletin,* Vol. I, No. 4, September, 1923; Vol. I, No. 1, January, 1923; Vol. III, Nos. 1 and 2, 1925.

NEW YORK CITY DEPARTMENT OF EDUCATION. Bureau of Attendance. *Annual Report of the Director of Attendance, 1914-15.* New York, 1916.

NEW YORK CITY DEPARTMENT OF EDUCATION. "Organizing the Work of Attendance Officers." In *14th Annual Report of the City Superintendent of Schools,* pp. 254-56, July 31, 1912.

NEW YORK STATE UNIVERSITY. *Census, Child Welfare and Compulsory Education Bureaus, Established 1917.* Bulletin No. 672. Albany, N. Y., The University of the State of New York, 1918.

NEW YORK STATE EDUCATION DEPARTMENT. *A Summary of the Compulsory Attendance Child Labor Laws of the States and Territories of the United States.* Bulletin 406. Compiled by James D. Sullivan. Albany, N. Y., State Education Department, 1907.

"New York's Parental School." *Harper's Weekly,* 54: 13, June 18, 1910.

NUDD, HOWARD W. *A Description of the Bureau of Compulsory Education in the City of Philadelphia, Showing How Its Organization and Administration Bear upon the Problems of Compulsory Education in the City of New York.* Public Education Association, 1913.

NUDD, HOWARD W. "How New York Registers Its Children." *Survey,* 27: 1777-80, February 17, 1912.

ODELL, C. W. "How Much Are Illinois Pupils Out of School?" *Elementary School Journal,* 24: 755-76, June, 1924.

O'HARA, EDWIN V. "The School Question in Oregon." *Catholic World,* Vol. CXVI, January, 1923.

OHIO SUPREME COURT. *Compulsory Education in Ohio. Patrick F. Quigley vs. The State of Ohio. Brief for Defendant in Error.* Columbus, Ohio, The Westbote Co., State Printer, 1892.

OPPENHEIMER, JULIUS JOHN. *The Visiting Teacher Movement with Special Reference to Administrative Relationships.* New York, Public Education Association of the City of New York, 1924.

PALMER, L. E. "New York's Truancy Problem." *Charities,* 15: 557-61, January 27, 1906.

PARKER, LA W. "Compulsory Education the Solution of the Child Labor Problem." *Annals o f the American Academy of Political and Social Science,* 32: sup. 57-66, July, 1908.

PAYNE, BRUCE R. "Educational Waste." *Atlantic Educational Journal,* 2: 7-9, 13, June, 1907.

PENNSYLVANIA, DEPARTMENT OF PUBLIC INSTRUCTION. Suggested Forms for Attendance Bureaus. 1922.

PENNSYLVANIA SCHOOL LAWS. *Digest of Laws Controlling School Attendance,* Department of Public Instruction, Pa., 1922.

PERRIN, JOHN W. *The History of Compulsory Education in New England.* Meadville, Pa., 1896.

PERRIN, JOHN W. "Indirect Compulsory Education, the Factory Laws of Massachusetts and Connecticut." *Educational Review,* 31: 383-94, April, 1906.

PHILADELPHIA, PA., BOARD OF PUBLIC EDUCATION. *Report of Bureau of Compulsory Education, 1916-18.* Philadelphia, 1917-19.

Philadelphia Survey. Board of Education, Philadelphia, Pa., 1922.

PHILLIPS, FRANK M. *Statistics of State School Systems,* Bureau of Education, Bulletin No. 31, 1921-22.

Proceedings, National League of Compulsory Educational Officials. Springfield, Mass., 1923.

Providence Survey. Board of Education, Providence, R. I., 1923.

ROBBINS, CHARLES L. *The School as a Social Institution.* New York, Allyn and Bacon, 1918.

ROTHERT, HENRY W. *Compulsory Education and Its Relation to the Defective Classes.* Council Bluffs, Iowa, School for the Deaf Press, 1904.

SHALLOW, EDWARD B. "Does a Strict Enforcement of the Compulsory Education Law Assist Teachers and Supervisors in Their Work?" In *National Education Association, Addresses and Proceedings,* pp. 1094-96, 1916.

SIMKINS, J. D. "Compulsory School Laws." *Ohio Educational Monthly,* 59: 335-41, July, 1910.

SLEED, ANDREW. "Compulsory Education." In *Southern Educational Association Journal of Proceedings and Addresses, 1904,* pp. 78-94. Also in *Southern Educational Review,* 2:376-93, October, 1905.

SMITH, D. V. H. "In a Truant School." *Living Age,* 272: 420-24, February 17, 1912.

SNEDDEN, DAVID and ALLEN, WILLIAM H. *School Reports and School Efficiency.* New York, The Macmillan Co., 1908.

SNEDDEN, DAVID. "Compulsory Attendance." In *Encyclopedia of Education,* edited by Paul Monroe, Vol. I, pp. 285-95; references, p. 295.

Springfield Survey. Board of Education, Springfield, Mass., 1923.

STATE LAWS ON COMPULSORY ATTENDANCE AND CHILD EMPLOYMENT. 48 States.

STRAYER, GEO. D. *Some Problems in City Administration.* New York, World Book Co., 1916.

STRAYER, GEO. D. and ENGELHARDT, N. L. *School Records and Reports.* New York, Teachers College, Columbia University, 1923.

STRAYER, GEO. D. and ENGELHARDT, N. L. *The Class Room Teacher at Work in American Schools.* New York, American Book Co., 1920.

STRAYER, GEO. D. and EVENDEN, EDWARD SAMUEL. *Syllabus of a Course in the Principles of Educational Administration.* Teachers College Syllabi, No. 11. New York, Teachers College, Columbia University, 1922.

STRUTHERS, ALICE and TROWBRIDGE, VERONA. "A Complete Attendance System." *American School Board Journal,* Vol. 69, No. 4, October, 1924.

SULLIVAN, JAMES D. "Compulsory School Attendance." In *New York State Education Department, 9th Annual Report, 1912.* Pp. 291-300. Albany, N. Y., 1913.

TEXAS, DEPARTMENT OF EDUCATION. *Compulsory School Attendance.* Bulletin No. 53, Austin, Texas, July 1, 1916.

TEXAS, UNIVERSITY, DEPARTMENT OF EXTENSION. PUBLIC DISCUSSION AND INFORMATION DIVISION. *Compulsory Education and Child Labor.* (Bibliography.) Austin, Texas, University of Texas, 1910.

TRABUE, M. R. *Measuring Results in Education.* New York, American Book Co., 1924.

"Truancy in Milwaukee: The Work of a New Kind of Truant Officer." *Survey,* 35: 637, February 26, 1916.

UNITED STATES BUREAU OF EDUCATION. "Compulsory Attendance Laws in U. S." In *Report of the Commissioner for the Year 1888-89,* Vol. I, pp. 470-531. Washington, Government Printing Office, 1891.

UNITED STATES BUREAU OF EDUCATION. "Compulsory Education and Child Labor Laws." In *Report of the Commissioner for the Year 1910,* pp. 148-53. Washington, Government Printing Office, 1910.

VAN SICKLE, JAMES H. "The Attendance Office." In his *Educational Survey of the Public Schools of Brookline, Mass.* Pp. 201-03. Published by the School Committee, 1917.

VIRGINIA PUBLIC SCHOOLS. *A Survey of a Southern State Public School System.* Part I. Yonkers, N. Y., World Book Co., 1920.

Visiting Teacher. U. S. Bureau of Education, Bulletin No. 10, 1921.

Visiting Teacher. U. S. Department of Labor, Bureau Pub. No. 53, April.

Watertown, N. Y., Survey. Board of Education, 1923.

WHITMAN, G. E. "A Continuous Census." *American School Board Journal,* March, 1925.

WILLIAMSON, JAMES W. "How Detroit Enforces School Attendance." *American Schoolmaster,* 13: 343-47, November 15, 1920.

WILSON, OTIS G. "Reliable Measurements of a School System." In *N.E.A. Journal of Proceedings and Addresses,* pp. 1067-69, 1916.

WISCONSIN. Education Laws, 1903, Chapter 349.

WOOLLEY, HELEN T. "The Issuance of Work Permits and Its Bearing on Other School Problems." *National Education Association, Addresses and Proceedings,* p. 489, 1915.

SUPPLEMENTARY

Annual Reports of Boards of Education.

Blank Forms obtained from all the cities visited and other cities.

INDEX

Date Due